Gru

Genesis of Hemispheres

IRIS SANKOH-DOUGLAS

THE CHOIR PRESS

First published in the United Kingdom in 2022 by
The Choir Press

ISBN 978-1-78963-270-5

Acknowledgements

To have arrived at this point is truly remarkable. This has been an epic journey for both myself, as well as a team of outstanding publishers. They are David Onyett, Rachel Woodman and Adrian Sysum of The Choir Press.

Everything I hoped and dreamt of has come true, from my initial tentative conversations about the possibility of having my work put into a book until this completed publication. The confidence instilled in me each time I spoke to a member of the publishing team, then the endless guidance and support throughout the editing of my manuscript, has given me so much. Professionalism, I always believed, is a chance to speak to a person, gain their advice then hear little or nothing from them again. The Choir Press have created a bridge making the impossible possible.

This first book is the gateway to a trilogy. Over the next couple of years I am going to take you with me on Orb's journey. From there, who knows? Whichever direction I choose to amble along, I wish to stay in the cosy home of The Choir Press, if they will keep me a comfy chair next to their hearts.

I also wish to thank Erbez Seferi. I work in a complex, and I am lucky enough to have Erbez as a manager. As I work the night shift my aim is to create a homely atmosphere. This I achieve by having a good work ethic and loving what I achieve. A community spirit keeps our team down to earth and humorous but professional, while working hard together. Teamwork is essential everywhere; it is the glue that sticks good ethics and good spirit together. An extremely supportive and forward-thinking head of operations is the secret ingredient in any organisation. My job at the complex is most definitely my home from home. So thank you, Erbez, for making menial work so enjoyable. Here is where I am reminded that this work is not just a job, but it makes the biggest difference to others' mental well-being.

I also wish to give gratitude to those 'unusual individuals' along my journey, that, unbeknown to them, forged the fibres of my unique tapestry, with their unwavering love, loyalty and weather-beaten wisdom. For it was they I required at those particular moments. It was they who left their indelible mark upon my soul. Because of my uniqueness, I choose to cherish those who have been, and are, set as jewels within the tapestry of my being. I choose to always enhance their lives, as they enhance mine, no matter how long the expanse of time. In choosing, I then allow myself to become a bridge that will join two worlds together. Hemispheres of consciousness that will, by their own architecture, give birth and nurture a new existence. I am eternally grateful for their existence, for possibilities of magic far beyond our universe.

Beyond the realms of thankfulness, the future awaiting only allows the brave insights to the unknown. I offer my humility to sacredness itself, in the understanding of a higher power. Upon all that has been, all that is and in the acceptance of all that is to come, I shall give of my best. For the betterment of this universe I shall live within the light of consciousness. All that I achieve I shall nurture to attain evolvement. Throughout the genesis of Orb, I will endeavour to illuminate those dark corners of our minds with compassion, with wisdoms, with gentility and with integrities formed from the ether of a child.

Namaste.

Freed

I dared to free my dreams like beautiful birds,
Then you found us and kept us safe.
Now we can see the whole universe
And live as stars in the night sky.
So all that glance our way
Shall never be afraid,
And so too let their dreams fly.

Dedication

This book has come into existence in order to create a consciousness of our universe. I dedicate Orb to my two incredible daughters.

With each breath, they lift me up into a beautiful universe. With every heartbeat, they show me how to fly. They are my Orb of sacredness. Hemispheres of infinite love and devotion. They illuminate my soul. They elevate my spirit. I am suspended within their consciousness. We are one being. We are a sphere of sacred spirits.

All that I am dwells within, beyond time and space.

All that they are I shall nurture and protect through all eternities.

They are my teachers of all wonderous things.

Enlightenments

I dreamt that one day
My soul would find
That sacred place
Where heart and mind
Could grow me.
Then you were born,
And I understood
What love meant
Because you both
Brought your light
So I could see.
And from your light,
I saw the meaning of love.
To have such grace,
To be so wise,
You both have flown
With magnificence
Brought from the sky.
I am so nurtured
With all you give.
By your ways,
You are my heartbeats,
You are the light.
So loved forevermore
In infinite,
In sacredness.
Within your magic
I shall live.
To find such love,
I am so humbled.

To know such wealth;
I am so blessed.
Now I am a warrior,
There is nothing less.
So know, my loves,
That I do see
How you both
Have set me free.
In all I do,
In all I say,
You shine your lights

You wait for me.
In the quietness of dreams,
When wishes are thrown
Upon the rocks of time.
You give me the best of you
Then wait to catch
My love, as angels do.
In the music of devotion,
You are symphonies
That fall down
From silvered skies.
And I then hear you
Through my darkest dreams.
You wait for me;
I hold your hands.
You always know
Just where I am.
You always grow
The best that I am.

Note From The Author

My name is Iris. I hail from Cardiff, born in the sacred grounds of Cardiff Castle.

I am the working mother of two incredible and adored daughters: working-class in its truest sense.

My father, a merchant seaman from Freetown, Sierra-Leonne, brought a uniqueness to my childhood I may not have experienced otherwise. He had the heart of a lion.

However, the gift of a loving mother was fleeting at birth. My father needed a mother to bring me up, but the woman he gave his trust to chose to abuse it.

I describe myself as 'the uniqueness from the alchemy of both love and hate', an impossible amalgamation of both sides of the human psyche.

Although raised by my adoptive mother, it was my father who is responsible for my strengths and universal ways of being.

This first book I have written is the figurehead to its trilogy. Orb is an eclectic mix of both poetry and vignettes of stories. Its atmosphere is one of possibilities. Our human condition will be questioned. Orb is the unseen entity of consciousness. In journeying through Orb's world, there is a chance to choose.

Universal in my approach, Orb speaks to the heart, addresses the ego, but most essentially translates emotions from the soul.

May this book be a source of spiritual strength. My wish for you is that you allow all that is sacred to nurture your world.

Namaste

Introduction

Orb is a consciousness of our sacredness.

This work that you have instinctively chosen, is a vignette of eclectic poems intertwined within a labyrinth of fact and fantasy.

Orb is the first of a trilogy. My wish for this voyage is that this is a journey of discovery for you.

In reading this book, all I ask is that you allow yourself to absorb the words. Leave perspectives in a quiet place. Find yourself a safe, cosy spot where you can have time alone.

Orb is about discovering the quiet place within ourselves. She has no expectations, no demands, no ego.

Her voice is one of positivity. Her language is universal. If you care to listen, you will hear sincerity in the echoes of her consciousness.

The human condition is complex; yet at its core, simplicity drives its engine. However, we find ourselves in a perpetuating cycle of confusion.

If through reading Orb an alternate consciousness arises, I am grateful.

Namaste

Within this book sleeps Orb.
If you choose to awaken her, possibilities will arise.
She may awaken you.

ithin This

As the sundial sheds its silhouette upon the passing of time,
We shed our beings upon the passing of our lives.
Need of fear is a dandelion shedding its seeds;
They will float whither they will.
No one can decide where they will fall.
So it is, your soul too shall be guided by nature from whence
    it came.
You will know when you are aligned with nature itself;
You can hear all the love from your heart and see all the
    beauty of your soul.

        Within this allowing myself to hear,
        I understood.
        Within this allowing myself to see,
        I discovered.
        Within this allowing myself to feel,
        I became alive.
        Within this allowing myself to heal
        I became strength.

Awaiting

So, hear my voice, for it has taken many years to speak.
We have lost our way upon this gentle earth.
If you hear, listen to your instincts, they are the portals of
our souls.
Do you not hear their cries amid perpetual storms of
ignorances?
They are waiting as a child to be born.
We have the choice to be all they need.

So, hear our voices.
We will interpret all language.
Our time is soon,
Then we will show the chosen.
Here this world shall be the place
Where every good will shall grow,
Where every evil has to perish.

Those who steal sacredness from the lost and abandoned
Gather all that is bereft without recompense
Then reap more than you could dare dream in the depths of
darkness.
Be more, and then again, become magnificence.
Live within your gifts, as they are alchemists of spirit.
Be harmony from the beauty and its beguilement.
Create its rhythms within the beatings of your heart.
Become vibrations of each breath throughout our universe.

I am a scar of countless wounds:
    Left bled of but hope.
        But this life was for a reason:
            To stand tall among inhumanities,
As a warrior girded against forces of fears and despair.

  Grow from the roots of desolation.
    Grow up through our abandoned earth.
        Walk with strength of soul
Upon this place where we were birthed.

Life flows within.
    Its sacredness adorns our form to see beyond this veil.
        Be not afraid of all that manifests upon our eyes;
            They are but phantoms of our selfishness
Come to take the souls of those who choose to take.

I breathe for you with courage of warriors,
    For you must rest now;
        You must rest content.
            Know your heart and soul are in my keep.

I breathe for this world that holds my life,
  Each breath a phoenix risen from the flames of ignorance.
    I breathe for children of our inspirations,
        Locked within the coldest corners of our disillusionment,
            That they may learn to fly into our sacred realms.

Allow those in our lives to choose whom they wish to be,
To live their own wisdom and integrity,
For they have been given their paths to choose,
Ours alone amid hellish minds and maladies.
And when we look upon who we really are,
We need no pain nor masks to wear upon our naked hearts.
Our fates await our loyal friends that guide as innocence
    sleeps within a child.

Return Into Light

Is truth a lie that hides just behind reality?
I make no sense of this our apparent disparity?
Does anyone really know?
Or are those that believe they do too afraid to show?
Truth is an endless road to journey when you're lost alone in
the dark.
You may wish life was within that pretty prism of
simplicities.
Can it be that there are no safe places to hide when you have
learnt abilities?
It is a force of nature too fast to catch with the human eye.
As much as it tears at your fears, live without becoming your
own worst slave.
Fear more the prison you have built while dying before you
have died.

Learn humility in life and all you live.
Open your mind to the infinite incredibilities within this
universe.
Be that child you once were with more beauty than any fear
could hold.
This is our journey of infinite steps we find waiting on our
paths.
Begin with this single moment of time.
See into that place where the door awaits.
It is carved with each stroke of your thoughts.
How you create your inner world will be its architect.
Walk with ease and gentility upon this earth.
Give reverence of deed through all your darkest days.

Be that which has been given to you from first you came.
There will follow beauty to protect breath and heartbeat.
Our journey is but short upon this vehicle of life.
We are allowed this space to be part of sacredness.
It is this gift that is what knowledge we all possess.
One life is a star that is here to light our way out of our
    ignorance.
Walk now; walk from this day with all the beauty that you
    are.
Humility will guide you when you become lost,
Infinite, with all the might and majesty within our mortal
    stars.

Sanctuary

Falling inside invisibilities of fluidity.
Whether I wish to move through these shards of colour,
    light, luminescence is of no concern.
Now there is only us amid echoes of energies: fast, swift
    encompassing energies.
They expand me far beyond human limitation,
Mind, body, head floating upon waves of warmth thrown
    down as if by magic.
My voice of intuition speaks: *You are with us now.*

Here arms surround me,
Precipice of a thousand depths,
To rest upon the heaviest of granite, eyes overlaid the
    bronzed horizon.
Unhurried, I earth myself again to feel the coastal path that
    melds like a silken serpent on weathered grass.
They give meditation to my impatient thoughts,
So here I seek no recollections of time that made
    impossibilities of rest.

Peacefully, I glance heavily at the waves that crash in
    tandem.
To be in company with this moment, albeit good, would
    allow the beast of distraction. And I do not wish to wake.
Each ethereal cloud detaches from the tranquillity of their
    turquoise.
My sight dissolves into its mercurial magnificence.
Effort has lifted as air that flows into each heartbeat.
Heavens merge with past and present amid dreams of a
    future fulfilled.

This memory of a summer's day has grown my soul.
My journey home did not wear nor worry me;
All passed too swiftly.
As the beauty of each bird, I realised that I too am nurtured
without knowing From which sacred place I did enter.
One thing is for certain:
I wish to return.

Reflection

I am the echoes that fall from your feet in an abandoned
  place.
I am a glimpse in the eye of a child with tears upon their
  face.
I am the touch that leaves a chill on your skin for a moment
  in time.
I am your longing when you discover a loss and discover it is
  divine.

I am a bird soaring where no man can dwell.
I am all heavens amid each and every hell.
I am the heart loving throughout eternities.
I am the day of new beginnings waiting to live free.

You are the book I read.
You are the nature that plants its seed.
You must grow strength to teach as a mighty tree.
You listen to your instincts, hold them in your care.
You are the Earth Mother.
You breathe life so that we live aware.

We struggle with passing of time;
We stumble throughout our egos;
We see only that which we choose to see.
Here, we are lost within a realm we should but know.
Reflections pull our thoughts
To and fro.
There is no sense in confusion.
Past comes to haunt us

In among times profusion.
Of memories we care not to keep,
Still they return
As lost sheep.
But there is no gain
In forgetting from whence you came.
So be not afraid
To hold the light.
For it is only your reflections
Looking back at you
From the mirrors of your mind,
From the shadows of your light.

Learning to Fly

As if night tears itself from day,
We struggle against all odds through life's decay,
Losing sight of what miraculous beings we really are,
Forsaking such possibilities awaiting.
Then who are we to say that pains need diminish such
    perfect gifts?
Each day our world is offered without recompense.

To learn to love,
To learn to fly.

Then who are we to tether that which is not ours
But has been created for all creation?
Then where do we learn to see
When we are blinded by our selfishness?
What then is this void that consumes us?
That which fills heart and mind so relentlessly?
Where then is our will to fly above this mortal realm and
    nurture all that is?

To learn to love
Is to learn to fly.

Being at One

Create from the broken pieces of our minds
Oneness that mends, so few can find,
History forever lost in time.
Faded fact or fiction, we may listen to their sounds, hear
    their stories.

I have looked beyond invisible realms;
Can you show me where to go?
    I have walked so far, there is no place here I do not know;
Will it never find my soulful heart?
    Because this pain will keep me true,
Though is it everything to be something other than you?

    Light that falls upon my steady stride,
Night that shades a place to hide,
    And all our worlds are lost to sight
If we no longer live to right such evil wrongs upon our hands.
    Listen while innocence pours in fathoms … like bloodied
    sands.

We are all the sum of our stars;
    Our lives and loves determined far beyond this universe.
As dust, we form to take our breaths within,
    To grow through all adversities if choice be ours.

From formed majestic and mighty rock,
  bejewelled from sacred fire and light,
    All worlds entwine to teach us the **unimagined**.
      For now is to listen with all our **faltered** eyes
        And silence that which has lost its way.

Today

Today is when we work together in lifting our hearts towards earth's light;

Today is when we teach each other in ways of understanding true meanings of life;

Today is when we walk together in the darkest of all storms and uncertainties;

Today is when we teach each other in ways of being everything we are meant to be;

Today is when we talk together amid our deepest pains;

Today is when we teach each other in ways of finding all love that remains;

Today is when we grow together in the confusion of our minds;

Today is when we teach each other in ways of humility from egos left behind.

Today is when we begin together in the nurturing of our universe.
Today we can walk;
Today we can work;
Today we can talk;
Today we can grow;
Today we can learn to know.
We are here for each other.
We are one.

Reach Outside

This life is about all of us.
Who? What? Where? Why?
We can wear that mask over our make-up?
But we may not like what we see.
Why not be the one who looks beyond
Places others would rather not be?
It is up to you
To break down those walls
That shelter you from all that is.
The face you see may frighten you
With its deceit and dark domains.
So if you dare break that first stone,
It may be
You will find
That you are not alone.
Then one day
When you are not aware,
Life will be waiting for you,
And as if by magic
You will discover
Who you really are.

Strange feeling when there's a price to pay,
I never understood what some people say.
It is like you have looked back,
And you see yesterday
Repeating itself today.

We have everything we need;
Still, some of us feel as if we have nothing,
Look without seeing,
Hear without listening,
Feel without connection to who we are.

Be the sound in an empty room,
Drumbeats from your soul.
Be the thought that translates vibrations.
It's in here!
Feel the trembling running through your fingers;
The life blood of countless beings.

Breathe with me!
This world,
This time,
This mind.
This heart is beating for all that is good:
The lost,
The poor,
The desolate of hope.

Then let us work together,
That which one can do
We can then all learn
Whichever way we choose.
It is not the paying of a price,
But the learning from our mistakes.
It is not the taking for a greed,
But the planting of a seed
Within a sacredness of mind.
We are the hope
Of our planet earth.
We are the dream
Of our countless
Children yet to come,
Our star angels
Born to shine as brightly as the sun.

Contemplation

In the space between thought and consciousness
Light enters.
It is an architect.
There we see what we create,
While our hearts appraise all that we wish.

We are hunters of our own pain.
Will we tear at the wounds of innocence?
Discard the bones of greed upon its bloodstain?

Call those you feel would aid you now,
As we are lost awaiting our demise.
She is waiting through ages, never fading.
Our faith in life shall shine its light upon our eyes.

Lift high, decaying insignificance.
I wish to live!
I wish to give!
Here dwells my Orb of infinities.

Should hell announce its bile and blood,
I stand as fortress against all foes.
Stance of heavens there remain untethered;
And there, as love endures,
Is everlasting.

Humilities

Tread upon this earth as a blessed soul.
You need not carry empty vessels which consume.
Lay sight as inspirations to those who have no love.

For I bear witness to all past,
Walked with ghost and gallant hearts,
Vanities and Valhalla of mortal loss born from the hand of
  eternities.

We are all the same,
Our lives interchangeable.
Perceptions converge; all memories align.
Absorb and refract limitations of maladies and mind.

Our hearts create our meaning.
We are all, and more, than we can dream;
Limitless horizons into other-worldly realms.

We are all the same,
For here is our beginnings,
Here there is no end.
One soul holds the light
For each to find their way.

Quietly the morning awakes
To look upon us as her children.
'Open your eyes,' she whispers.
'I will help you grow.

'Come walk with me today,
All our world is waiting.
Come talk with me and play,
This is our world to nurture.'

In the sky float all of the wishes and dreams of each child.
Every good thing that is given is a seed that will grow.
In our world someone gives love;
Somewhere soon someone else's love will grow.
And the more you can love from the depths of your heart,
Our world will heal, and from there we can start.

The Art of Growth

To awaken with the dawn's bright shadows, before the sun lifts her head and unfolds sleep from our mind. To catch each morning: morning dusted with hope, curiosity and, of course, love, because love is necessary to create, nurture, protect and grow everything. Nurture seeps into the soft fibres of billions of grains of energy that make up existence: life fibres that breathe, eat, drink. In fact, nurture is the very essence of the most beautiful forms of life; plants, rocks, humans—everything there ever was or is—grow in a fabulous way because of this magical ingredient: love.

The art of growth is a tricky business, to be sure. Not much is as it seems—something discovered on my unequipped journey of self-discovery. Life really is what you work hard enough to make.

As a child, my need was to give. That giving had no desire for something in return. I felt somewhere that no words would, or could, be interpreted through the labyrinth of tangled emotions. There was an agenda, powerful and inexplicable in ways I did not need to understand. Being free to share this precious jewel that was my creativity was all I needed to know. Having just the basics of life was to be invited into a toy shop. I discovered how little wealth and its abundance mattered in the world of children—any child.

Life is all-encompassing. This experience is what we make of it. From my realisation that I was in this experience, I moved with a purpose. A day to me was an opportunity to give something extremely important of myself. There had to be a powerful reason for this gift of time to be given to me. Within my child ways there was always an unrelenting force of nature, a compulsion to create wonderment that was tactile and colourful and that furnished those places with something inexplicable but nurturing—something invisible that transformed the original energies with good emotions. It was of no consequence that I was a child; this way of being was, and is, who, or what, I am. Whatever the circumstances, life for me is where my soul can journey throughout this home. Upon this journey I can create good energies to achieve wonderful things. It is a synergy. It is a synchronistic language I have a universal power to speak.

Through the art of growth there is that choice we are adept at communicableness. How we choose to use this ability is a contentious question. The actions speak from your deeds, as it were. Negative ways of being create loss of creativities. They absorb good in subliminal ways. They hide inside happiness and gnaw away at beautiful intentions. Lives, families, jobs and communities are like vulnerable children to its dark apothecary. So here, as everything that we believe we have control over, is where our existence is more, much more, inexplicable than we dare to imagine.

Become

Selflessness.
Become humility
When you are consumed with self,
For there you will learn understanding.

Become tranquillity
When you are as a storm of rage,
For there you will learn gentleness.

Become compassion
When you have become vengeance,
For there you will learn forgiveness.

Become strength
When you have become weakness,
For there you will learn courage.

Become knowledge
When you have become ignorance,
For there you will learn wisdom.

Become infinite
When you have become insignificance,
For there you will learn magnificence.

Become consciousness
When you have become hate.
Here you become love.

Funny Stuff

Words have the power to destroy or create,
Repeat or alter fate,
Build love out of materials of hate.
Dog-walking on a rainy day,
When those who cannot go out require a helping hand;
Garden tidying while keeping their resident cat company;
Surprise because it could not have been planned.
Cats are their own peoples.
They got plans:
They like to watch beatles
And little things that hop and crawl.
Plenty make homes in your garden walls,
Scuttling along your garden paths,
Bugs are genius at arts and crafts.
Cats, on the other hand,
Will never tolerate cold things,
Especially when there is a chance
Of a bumblebee dance
On your favourite jumper.
They wouldn't wish for
Anything less lumpier.
Always know where there's a fluffy hat,
A colourful, abandoned scarf.
It's theirs for the snuggling.
Takes a lot of cheek, you know,
To take up residence inside your furry coat,
A warm abandoned duvet,
An open door into your bedroom,
Always gratefully accepted.
With a cheeky grin,

And force-ten purring,
You'd kick yourself
If you didn't leave them in.
Oh yes!
Of course, couldn't live with yourself.
The guilt.
The shame.
All-consuming blaming,
You are no more
Than a gibbering wreck;
But what the heck!
You are loved,
More than you could ever dream.
And be assured,
Life will never again be lonely.
As your house will be a home,
You then will know what love really means:
Belonging.

Sleep has a colour.
It may be light;
Then again, it could be dark.
Most times it sticks on things
When you're not looking.
Busy days make great colours
That flow through your mind,
And as soon as you stop,
Sleep jumps out from the clock.
'There she is!'

You can't run,
You can't hide.
You just have to flop;
Time for bed has arrived.
Hot cocoa inside,
All the noise turns to nought.
So many things you've been taught
Have been swept away into your happy place.
Yes, when all's said and done,
Your world will always be functional.
Rest now to be strong for your next incredible day.

Time crawls upon the hands of clocks and collects our
    memories.
They slide into baskets left in corners of our minds.
Thoughts stumble down slippery staircases of silliness
Puddled on sparkly floors washed clean of recollections.

Bedtime is a place where today melts into tomorrow.
Serenely sleeping on our intricate fabric of time and space.
It finds its own place with a shove and a push,
Like a smile creeps up on a happy face.
You never had to call it;
You never had to pay.
But now it has arrived,
You just want every bit of it to stay.

It is all about belonging,
Nothing else would ever do.
When you give
With all your heart and soul,
Beautiful things,
Will forever return to you.

Orb's Awakening

Bedtime, after all, is where we dream. Tomorrow whispers exciting secrets that no one knows how to find. Even the skies hide new days in case there are those who cannot wait to try to sneak a peek. So as not to leave us in the dark, stars are thrown and scattered across the sky. If we look long enough, they wink, as if to say 'I see you too! Goodnight, little ones!'

Everything turns to hush on the countdown to bedtime. Those bits and pieces of stuff that has filled up the day like a pile of old clothes making their home in an abandoned cardboard box. Changed out of your day clothes, a bath or a shower, a splash in the sink. Frames of time caught our movie of us. A slow walk around the park, snatch a taxi, grab a bus. I wonder, in our worldly sea of suburbia, how each drop of us makes all the difference. This day, as all, must be loved and cherished: put safely away until needed again quite soon. To dream is where we can be taken to another world, to find that which has been lost, to return to where we know our purpose. This world of dreams takes us on extraordinary journeys that are specific only to ourselves. This was Orb's time to dream.

***

'We kept a blanket for you, as we knew you would join us.' Orb was handed a downy, red blanket that when picked up doubled in size. There was a big yellow flower stitched onto it. It had the appearance of being alive. She had no idea what flower this was, but it reminded her of home. 'Cuppa hot chocolate, Orb?'

'Yes please!' she replied, and swooped across, winged and beautiful. The over-large mug made itself fit into her petite, eagled hands. Steam floated into the warm evening breeze. Quietness wrapped itself around all that came to be. A roaring crick-crackling fire danced with crimson flames swathed with ambered logs, which refracted upon the night's rich canopy, smudging it with an eerie murmuring of midnight shadows and mysterious majesty.

'Who needs help for our newest day, everyone?'

Orb gazed around the fire in excitement as she realised a circle of fabulous friends had gathered and were splendid. Her mind confirmed, *These are all my friends who came to be with me tonight.* Although they all looked quite different, they strangely all looked the same—as if they had come from the same place but had different jobs to do.

As one stood, her legs seemed to go on forever. Fingers tapered down into nails resembling eagles' talons. Clothed in metallic scales that shimmered and glinted as rainbows colliding down into a fountain.

'At last! Indeed! We have been here all along! Now is truly a magical evening. This meeting, this night, has often been discussed by us, your guides. But then I suspect you have always known of us. From that cold winter's day when you were brought into this world of humans, we have watched, influenced and protected you.

'We chose a gentle woman whom we knew to have the special instincts to raise you well, although it proved to be too dangerous to leave you with her, as she was not given her place to grow and create balance for you to be nurtured as so required.

'From that moment, you were at risk. Your life became unbalanced at the whims of those who were given your charge. Your father was in place to keep you close in his protective care. A substitute mother had to be put into place. We, as your outer-world guardians, had no other choice but to stand back, as it was your father who chose your mother.

'Years now you have had to endure many and much suffering. Throughout this you have not let go of your instincts.

'Even in these dark, dark times you have chosen to nurture the female that has given you no compassion, who chose to deny you happiness rather than create and sustain it. You, Orb, have given where no one else would give. You, Orb, have created and sustained a loving, compassionate home. You, Orb, are life without pain, giving without taking, happiness without despair.'

Orb felt her eyes full of heavy tears and wondered just what she was supposed to do now. Everything had fallen upside down. She had no idea how to begin to find which way was up.

Her lips had no real purpose it seemed. Words were too small, too insignificant, for such an incredibly bewildering event.

'Do you wish to speak, my child? We are here for you.'

As the gathering of beguiling and Etherial beings waited silently, they then began to stand up. One by one they started to chant in a most beautiful and mesmerising unified wave of sound. The enormous oaks that grew all around looked as if they had walked there, choosing to shield this special place to protect everything in it. Then the earth began to pulsate in time with the chants.

Beautiful animals arrived along with birds. From the corner of her eye Orb was aware that the fast-flowing stream had stopped flowing. There had fallen a silence.

A footstep away stood this lithe, elegant, what looked to be, wood nymph. This was the being that spoke to Orb when she first arrived. Now she could see closer the feathers that adorned her body. They were metal! They quivered with the vibrations of the deep, rhythmical notes. Her eyes were extremely large, with two irises of different colours: the inner as if silver, the outer as if rainbows. On each side of her head stood antennae which possessed the ability to retract when required. It was all so unbelievable to Orb, but there held a familiarity to this place. How and why, she knew not. So it was, that Orb had visited many times throughout her mysterious life.

When Orb was seven, or thereabouts, she had been told she was adopted. This was only explained to her because she had had an argument with a school friend one afternoon while visiting at the weekend.

'She's not your mother!' shouted Maya.

'Yes she is. You are a liar! And this is not kind of you!' shouted Orb.

'So, you just go ask your mother then!'

Immediately, Orb ran into the room next door, where her mother was chatting to Maya's mother.

'Mum! Mum! Maya says that I have no mother – that I am adopted! What is adopted, Mum?'

Orb's mother stared at her in an uneasy silence and looked at Maya's mother with fear in her eyes. Maya's mother looked sad, and her eyes filled with tears that seemed to fill her with pain. Maya dropped her head as if it had succumbed to gravity.

'Yes!' Maya screeched.

'Why didn't you tell her? demanded Maya's mother.

'She didn't need to know.'

The reply filled the room with the most intense sorrow. Orb was left in its mist, lost, confused, her heart torn into a million pieces and thrown into a raging storm.

***

From then on, each day carried a strangeness with it that would not find a safe and peaceful shelf on which to sit. Nothing would translate this cruel language for even Orú to understand. But then, Orú possessed a gentility that shone as a beam thrown out by the biggest lighthouse. No matter how desolate and desperate people proved themselves to be, Orú would see straight through their most evil ways of being. Whenever animals came around they instinctively knew they would be safe and nurtured. Anything or anyone that would not be able to give good of themselves could not stay around Orú. She held a presence that was all sacred and magical. Orú was Orú.

Growing up she endured school because she had to. That was what others did. To be the same requires a conforming that loses you within its make-up—a mask that has to be worn as a matter of course. Most days she ran and ran, even if she had no need to. Some had no real anchor as to how they came into existence.

No matter what, her father had been there with her all along. To some there was no father figure within her life. Not living in her household, but a two-hour journey away in another city, he was a merchant seaman for most of his life. When time arrived, his health had weakened. Then he worked as a railway cargo loader—bleak, cold, damp, relentless and cruel to the spirit. That worn-and-torn oilskin jacket he wore never did keep out the weathers, only etched him away each night until he became almost invisible. His soul became invisible. Visits to her father came at the cost of many hours of heartache and longing for the father she loved more than her heart could hold. School holidays were the only allotted time they could spend together, when she could breathe and wish to take that next breath. Promises of time with her father, to go and visit friends of his or just time to spend exploring wherever time allowed. Once again, Orb would always be who she was meant to be: nurturing. Dreams that Orb had dreamt came and went with their familiarity. The same dreams. Recollections of vivid colours, sounds that were unearthly, visions of extraordinary beings. An extraordinary world that transported her to an enchantment of her senses within a wood. She knew she was different – that was instinctive – and that was how she wished to be.

Upon small hours of Orb's dream state she entered once again into this familiar world. Colours from a fire painted walls of the enormous room with sinuous shapes. The moon reflected her icy, silvered, mercurial splendour onto large, bowed glass windows. Dancing silver polka dots swiftly swam across any dark shadows that shrouded a great castle just on the edge of her eye. Orb did not know whether she was dreaming or if she was just somewhere she had wished to be, imagining through her mind's eye. Imagination is a most powerful and perceptive gift of Orb's. Ticking, ticking. A clock from the far corner of her room. She turned and sat upright from her restless slumber to listen. Her bed quivered and felt as if it had landed from some other-worldly planet. Looking down, she shuffled back with a gasp that was neither alarm nor fear. Her bed was sparkling and glittering beneath a beautiful orange, silken quilt. Diamond stars were embedded in clusters here and there. It was the night sky. It was on her bed!

Stepping out of her bed, she could see the entrance to a corridor that had appeared from nowhere. There was the softest, safest feeling beneath her feet. A sapphire-blue carpet began to unfurl ahead of her footsteps.

'I am in the sky!' she exclaimed.

At the end of this corridor that drifted and flowed like a gently flowing river waited a room with no apparent walls. Around and about were fabulous pieces of furniture; sturdy, carved, oaken barrels; funny-shaped jars filled with soft pastel colours of unusual things; and sweets or home-made cakes, so she hoped – whatever they were they looked scrumptious! There, across the vast room, towered a stack of freshly chopped wood which smelt of cinnamon and honey. Moving as if floating, she could hear the tick, tick once again, only this time she had a sense that whatever it was, it was not a clock. There were no clocks!

Each step. Tick, tick! Pause. Silence. Then Orb gazed over a gnarled, knotty, busy set of bookshelves. There, was the largest, greenest, most wonderful cricket she had seen in her most unusual life.

'It's me!' chirped a happy, high-pitched voice.

'Who's me?' puzzled Orb.

'Tick-Tick! Me!'

'Have you come to keep me company?'

'Why wouldn't I?' answered the cricket in a very matter-of-fact manner. 'In case you're wondering, or even totally baffled, this is Etherialah! Here is where dreams come true!'

'Thank goodness! I have arrived at last! It is as if I have been longing to be here forever. Now I know I have known this place forever. I can finally feel at home.'

'Of course! Why wouldn't you know this place? This *is* your home, Orb! This is where you belong. Those places you were searching to find your home could not be for you. You are meant for other such things. Destiny was ordered for you to be a creator, not a destroyer. In such a manner there is a way of being. More will be told in given time. My words now are to welcome you, beloved Orb.

'Here you will have love, nurturement, time and protection to grow into that which is destined. Here all is. From this, all that is sacredness will grow.'

Time stood still. A feeling of serenity held Orú with such peacefulness, that she had, for the first time, a complete sense of belonging. Kindness would be all and everything unto this realm now that Orú had found what she really was. She realised she was smiling. In that smile she could see everything from her past. It all made perfect sense. At that time there was no feeling, only a heart that was too big and pain that used to be so much bigger. From that moment, Orú was content with what she was.

As she raised her head to look up at Tick-Tick, the room filled with a multitude of fabulous beings like nothing she had ever experienced before. They spoke a language that was incomprehensible to her. Something was about to happen. She could feel it. She was born to be here, in this magical, beautiful place.

Tick-Tick explained, 'These words are ancient speak. They tell of that which has and will come to pass within worlds that wait upon the edge of time. We are here because this is your time. Many moons ago we gave you to the humans to nurture and raise for an allotted span in their years. Through our understanding of how and why humans decide to live by the laws they choose, we have decided that your earth time must now be concluded. You have dealt enough with these misgivings. Now it is so! You, Orú Etherial, have much work to do in this, our, world. All that you have learnt there will be put to great use. Nothing has been lost, innocent one. In the world of humans you kept yourself with incredible purities of that which you are. Every day you have emanated the light of the highest orders of our angels. There this has healed and restored the souls of all those who have walked in your presence. Those who choose to walk within the darkness do so forever and will not absorb this light. They are lost to this sacredness here. This undoing can only reveal itself by the mightiest of deeds. You, Orb, are to return to us now. Our realm is in need of you. We are the guardians of all sacredness! This is full enough for that time. We are in need of you now. It is time for you to become that which you are. All here must walk, talk, speak, hear and know your nurturement.

'From where you have left is to be as night fallen into emptiness. But all is to be waiting, but not lost. Here, now, what was lost to us is now returned for eternities once more. Tomorrow our celebrations shall be prepared for your star-building ceremony. Our gathering is a oneness within thought, mind and action. We have the powers to undo ill will in all and everything throughout all times. We are the guardians that are the gatekeepers to infinities—that which has been and always shall be.'

Orb's head began to feel so heavy that it slipped down onto her heavy arms. Her eyes shone softly, gently closing as if the weight of all that had happened was absorbing her into this beautiful dream. Tick-Tick smiled at the sacred assembly that had come to welcome Orb home, and they all bowed before her as they did upon her departure.

'Peace be upon you, Orb Etherial! Yes! You are here with us, returned home. We have met many times throughout your years within the human world. Within your sleep I have visited with words from our world. Your dreams were the bridge to our world from where you came and belong: dreams that were sent to remind you that we are here waiting for your return. It has been an immensely long and arduous journey for such a sensitive Orb as you. Because of this way of being, our most elite and powerful warriors have been assigned to your protection. Upon this, your home world, we have evolved through fearsome and fascinating journeys, some which have discovered magic and mysteries that we, as wise as we are, could never have imagined possible. Throughout this era you have always grown with our principles of nature and fortitude, always loving, always giving of yourself. So we have returned to bring you back to your world of Etherials, to which you are daughter of our queen. Orb, you are our child. Chosen to become enlightenment of the realm of humanity. Tonight is to be the 'undoing ceremony', where all ill will given shall be undone. This is your ceremony, Orb. Each deed of love, devotion, sacrifice and enlightenment bestowed has come full circle. And so, you must be. Thus, here you will explore and restore past and present to ensure that which has been nurtured will be so.'

As Tick-Tick took her gentle hand, a purring sound came from somewhere out of sight. Within the shadows of oaken pillars stood what looked like a dragonfly. Huge eyes, the colour of emeralds, glinted across at Orb with the most loving gaze. A silvered body, tall as the tallest of horses. To gaze upon this wonder was to be in awe.

Orb could hear words fill her head, but she could not see anyone speak them. 'All that you have has given you all the wisdom you require for our tasks ahead. Each day, each sadness, has not been wasted as you may have believed. This was as necessary as the air is here for us to breathe. As water has formed upon this planet, so we may sustain many life forms. As this earth bears us its flora and fauna within which we are given our homes, everything has a place amid a purpose of this in our world. Humans have a need to possess that which must not be possessed; it is inherent within. Yet there are those in nurturing places who are not typical; they are aware. All that they are is within their field of consciousness. These individuals choose specific ways of life. Life for them must be a conscious path. This path is decided by the elders, and it is through them alone that the laws of this realm of humanity are watched over. Humans would call us angels. We are armies that ensure that that which must be shall be. There is, unknown to most, such a place within our domains that is a place of undoing. Those of heart and mind of desolation will be forever without substance. Nothing will grow or be nurtured amid their barren souls. For us, the Etherials, all is to be balanced with nature. She is our Earth Mother; from her we all are nurtured. Our warrior angels do not allow those of destruction to pursue those who must be protected, for they have chosen, and through their gift of choice they have doomed themselves to eternal abandonment by all things sacred.

'Your dreams, our sacred child, from the past, here in the present and awaiting future, are our portals to your subconscious. The world of physicality is a mere facade of illusions that once discovered dissolves as smoke upon a sleeping lake. We have heard your cries through your darkest, loneliest nights, as a child calling for her mother. We have watched you battle through your war of survival from the beginnings of your handing over until now. We have felt your inconsolable pains cut through our realm until we would allow no more. These times had to be worn like an ill-fitting garment, all that you possessed in this world. You have now understood the words of our wise; now you understand. You alone have crawled through each hell, scarred and bloodied, and have become a warrior. You have evolved. Here is your home: Etherialah. Each sunrise for you has been shadowed by cruel and false entities. Where each desolate seed remains to rot and decay, you, Orb, have become the forest of a thousand trees. You, Orb, have been chosen to teach and guide our armies to nurture and protect those who are creators on this human plain. Such worthiness is only bestowed upon once in a millennium to those who are with sight.

'Long ago ancients evolved from our star system possessing incredible and indescribable powers. While these powers were fabulous and held untold potentials, only those worthy could understand how to use them for the good of all. Their powers would then become a force that would heal as if invisible to those without this knowledge. So, in the billions of star systems, Etherials gathered the knowledge within the wisdom of sacredness itself. There was and is none other than they. We are star warriors. This is your birthright. This is who you are, my beloved child.'

Music bubbled along the tips of the great oaks. They had turned a rich shade of purple with the moving of the night. Orb's eyes caught sight of a glowing within the forest clearing. A swarming of humming birds perched upon the rise of the crooked stone bridge that crossed over a luminous river just on the brow of the forest's ridge. She blinked as if she did not believe what was before her. As the melody floated around, the smell of scented flowers wafted like an ocean wave. Everything began to sway to a melodic vibration she had heard once before. It was as if this was a universal language for this magical world Orb was now at one with. Where the sun had set that day rose a chanting that made the ground pulsate in a peculiar manner. Countless eyes were watching, mesmerised by the knowledge of what was to come. Glinting silver, an army appeared as if one machine. Swords and shields undulated upon beautiful chiselled armour that sang across the perfumed dusk of that enchanting night. Fires stacked with logs glowed and crackled all about the clearing with fantastic beings sitting. Uniquely designed jewelled colours, that were rain, bowed within Orb's eyes. She could not stop smiling but had no idea this was where she had wanted to be the whole of her life. It seemed every being was watching her.

'Who are they all?' asked Orb.

'They have come to meet you, Orb; come to show you that you are their queen warrior. We have been waiting so long. This is for you, our ceremony of return for one who we have dedicated our lives to,' explained Tick-Tick. 'Among them your sisters and brothers. They too are warriors within our realm's armies. We will lay down our lives in all lifetimes for you, our daughter of Zauz, our sacred father and warrior. You see that warrior in the centre of the clearing circle?'

'Yes!' replied Orb.

'That is your father, Zauz. He has watched over you from the day you were born.'

As they watched, her father began joining the head of the procession of warriors. His armour was studded with jewels on one side, and a scarlet was cloak draped over the other. He looked wise and powerful. He glanced across at Orb with the gentlest of smiles she had ever seen. In the blink of an eye, the long snaking ranks had stopped just a few steps away with a thunderous cry: 'Orb, our queen!'

A single female warrior walked towards Orb with outstretched hands. The glint of a beautiful sword filled Orb's whole being with a power she had not known. She accepted.

Then her father spoke. 'We, the Etherials, became enlightened through many moons of learning the ways of our ancestors. We were given this before the beginnings of time, to be the light-givers of all universes. Through this we have become guardians for the sacred realms. I, your father, am whole once more in this gift of all gifts: your return. See now your sister, captain of our sacred armies. She is Ithean, one who protects. Your brother, Zein, commands the alliance armies that also are the guardians of our divinities of universe. Here we must remain in this sacred world, for we protect all that is within eternities and that which shall be. Since your arrival you have become aware that all here is far from ordinary.' Pointing, Zauz glanced towards a oneness of incredible beings just on the edge of Orb's right line of vision. 'These are the love and devotion from thoughts, hopes, wishes, deeds and inspirations of every beautiful-souled being from infinite realms. Soul guardians that create and nurture everything magical that manifests within each and all, nurtured in such a way as not to be seen or imagined. This is magical. But by this magic an awareness of that which is sacred is seeded. So by this is born principles of how they need to live in dignity, within a love of all life, through giving all of that bestowed upon creation itself. In building with love, they will then understand why we are here.'

As if in a dream, beings of spectacular shapes, colours and sounds began their procession through the glowing clearing of the woods. It was as if the sun had descended amid this fantastical spectacle, chanting what sounded like a language from another world. Loud, hypnotic sounds sounding like her name! It was! It was Orb's name!

'That's my name!' Orb exclaimed.

'Yes!' replied her father. 'Every being here has longed for your return, my child.'

'I believed I was abandoned in this world,' whispered Orb. 'Never fitting in anywhere! No one seemed to know how to treat me, or care. Now I am me! You are the father I have always dreamt of! Thank you! For being my father!'

Zauz laughed, threw his arms—powerful arms—around

Orb, then picked her up, holding her safe to his heart. Her sister and brother came to join them both to complete the circle. A great 'Hoorah!' filled the air and rainbow-coloured flowers danced through the scented evening.

'Where is my mother?' implored Orb.

'Your mother is on her way home to us, angel. Others in our realms have need of her. She is the nurturement mother of all that is and ever shall be. Your mother is highest of sacredness. Sacred guardians are the highest of our realms and are needed for all beings wherever they are, whatever their need. All are tended to with love and integrity, so that those fierce and fiery forces of life shall be overcome, transported to those places where light, wisdom and love is forever to remain.'

Orb was in need of a moment, for her mind was filled with abundance, far beyond that which she could fit into her petite little head. Orb looked at her sister, caught her hand and said, 'Please could I sit down, just for a moment?'

Her father and brother were smiling: a knowing smile that reassured their new-found sister that she would never be afraid ever again. 'Come! Come on, our child of change! We have great things to achieve! First you are to be returned, in this our ceremony of sacredness, to your mother who has waited within the corridors of the "ages of resolutions". The robe of rebirth is prepared for you, Orb Etherial. Only you are able to wear this. As too for your sister and brother, these garments are living entities which possess each attribute you have acquired throughout your life. These are part of you throughout your life. *You* strengthen these garments as *they* strengthen you. One day they shall both meld as one. As the forger melds within the swords they build with sweat and strength, foresight of wisdom waits. Therefore, with creation of love and integrity, holds too its maker's courage. As we are to begin celebrations to honour Orli, our daughter of wisdom, we join hands as one being. Though wise through infinite pains of wounds too deep to see, your wisdom is now to flourish within all realms, in order to uncover the lost light. Orli is here! We are complete!'

There came a roar so deep that it rumbled inside the great trees, through the dark, heavy, rich earth, high into the very night that draped this magical miracle, as this night was long awaited. This night was where the very essence of nurturement, of sacredness, was to be. No one could stand still, or wanted to. This was to be breathed in like a warm, heady breeze that filled their energies with a life force that could never end. Laughter trickled along lips, rested upon eyes that sparkled with hopes, dreams, longings of worlds within universes that dream of what can be.

'Sire! Sire!' A tall, elegant guardian soldier holding a scroll strode across to Orli's father announcing his queen had just arrived and was being transported to them as they spoke.

'I am to leave a short time to join with our queen. Keep my child safe, Ealion. I shall return with my lady swiftly.'

As Orli vanished towards the sacred ring of oaks, she turned back to her father, sighing.

'My father! My sister! My brother! To be reunited with my sacred mother!'

***

So many wonderful times to live. Home now, for always. Never to leave or be apart from her beloved family ever again, Orli was content.

In a short while, while celebrations were filling her eyes and head with the most fantastical visions she had witnessed before, there fell a hush. Everything stood silent, with the sky changing to a beautiful lilac. Birds of many colours glided past in formation, as if they had been waiting for this hallowed moment. Light appeared from the depths of the great forest. An emerald-green beam pierced through trees, leaving all the air shimmering with silver mist. A chariot pulled by seven horses covered in silvered armoury trotted to a stop a few feet away from Orb.

'Hello, my beloved daughter! I have so missed you. It was my voice you heard upon your arrival.'

Orb tilted her head in amazement and looked up at this incomprehensible sight that addressed her with such gentleness.

'I am Earths, your mother. All you see, and all that is, is our home. We are guardians of sacredness itself. You have been brought home to us, where you can now create all that you are for the good of all.'

Earths looked like a fantastical humming bird because of her suit of armour. It was metal scales of an incandescence of colours that pulsated as if breathing.

'How amazing!' gasped Orb.

'Yes, I believe so!' replied Earths, smiling adoringly at Orb.

'You have come to take me to the Circle of Sacredness,' said Orb in a matter-of-fact way.

'You are knowing, Orb,' replied her mother. 'We are now connected, and this can never be broken. Since the moment you were carried back home to us, we have been mind–body connected. In the world of humans we had only mind connection with you. This time has passed, as is known. You are once again restored to us and our realm. Come now! Go with these two warriors. They will take you to our castle, to the Hall of Dreams. There, you will be robed for your ceremony.'

'Are you not coming with me, Mother?' asked Orb quizzically.

'We are always with you, my child. We shall be waiting at the castle. You will be joining us all to forge your strength with guardian elders, so that we will be as one in the halls of our universes.'

'What is that?' whispered Orb.

'All questions shall become answers, my angel of our realms. Fear not from this place on. You are now within our inner sanctum of guardians, to be loved, to be the breath of our worlds. Fear has no existence within these realms; it is a long-passed relic of human incomprehensions. Our warriors fear nothing, as they are all that is. They see that which cannot be seen. They hear that which cannot be heard. They feel that which cannot be felt. You will only know love and be taught how to nurture your sacred abilities for the good of everything.'

With that, two warriors took Orb's little cloth bag which she wore across her back, her most precious possession in her lonely life as a child. One bowed, offering up his gauntleted hand to her to come with them. Graciously, he lifted Orb up upon a beautiful horse that had been specially armoured with bejewelled, scaled plates and a purple saddled harness, which was Orb's favourite colour. He made her safe and told her she would always be safe and that they were her personal warriors and they would do anything and forever be hers to be called upon at any given time. Upon opening the door that was as silver as silver can be, Orb stepped into a room as endless as a horizon. Windows climbed upwards, reaching for sky and light. They were framed in purple swathes of velvet tumbling into puddles of softness upon the granite floors. Warm woods dressed everything about this magnificent chamber: Orb's chamber. Night had begun to throw its moonlit glow through the stained glass, leaving everything ghostly shimmered in the fire glow that bled from the centre of the stone hearth.

Following a path of ambered light, Orû walked slowly, her heart feeling strange, yet stronger than ever. Her eyes were drawn to the dancing flames that played and tumbled across the big logs that glowed ruby red with amber flecks. Orû was home. Such a peace here that she had ever known in her entire nurturing life.

'Orû of ancient prophecy!' echoed a loud voice from the darkened corner. 'Beloved child of this guardianship of sacredness, you are she of whom we have spoken of for many ages within all dreams and imagination. You of whom we have waited throughout times beyond time. Our world holds you within its nurturement. We hold all that is sacred in all realms and are now in preparation to complete our "age of wisdoms". Here shall be your ceremony of the universes! This is where you came each night in your dreams. We all heard you! We all saw you! You are our child! We move as one entity. We are the sacredness of all and each world before time, as time, beyond time. There can be no time unless we are present to nurture and protect every being. This is your birthright!'

The soft candlelight that had draped upon the ancient, earthen stone walls was suddenly pierced with sharp beams of flickering torchlight. Great silvered doors slowly waved open. Seven female warriors marched through. Silence was all to be heard. Tall and with turquoise armour, gleaming and undulated with colours that reflected their heat from the huge hearth which looked like a fiery portal to other worlds. Three-tiered wings cascaded around their shoulders, moving, moulding themselves in harmony with each and every other soldier. Shadows flew around the muted, dusky stone, giving life to the beauty of inanimate objects surrounding the chamber. Their sculptured wings weaved through their flowing purple hair. The air filled with a strange humming and the smell of magnolias.

All along, the door to this world was waiting to be unlocked; now it would be forever in Orb's keep.

'They come here to escort you to the sacredness tonight, Orb,' explained her mother, whose voice spoke into Orb's mind as if she herself was there. 'First they will prepare your bathing place. Then they will robe you in your armour and all that is required for your ceremony. This night you shall be evolved into our realms of universes upon the seventh hour. From there we become complete with all!'

The warrior guard beckoned to Orb, and two approached her, taking her into the bathing chamber.

'Come, Orb!' they spoke softly. 'Let us make all special for your arising of our enlightenment time!'

From the preparations, Orb was now fully armoured with a beautiful strength that shone like a beam of light from her eyes. A glass tower reflected its outline past the full moon so endlessly that it seemed it was the sky itself. Moonlight had seared itself on everything with a majestic iridescence too fabulous to find words worthy enough to utter. Music drifted upon the branches. Orb had been seated on a red toadstool. Her father appeared at her side.

'You have come to keep me company, Father,' said Orb.

'Your sword, my child,' replied her father.

Orb smiled a loving smile, rose up with her father and walked to the Throne of Enlightenment.

As in her dreams, Orb had finally come home.

Lights of beautiful colours poured out of this new and magical sky of stars, planets and universes of fantastical beings of Orb's realms of incandescence. She was now high guardian warrior.

Queen Earths, mother of Orb, smiled as she had never smiled before. All was well within her domains for many purple moons before. That night of Orb's evolvement ceremony would hold the fibres of every world in its silent care. The procession of the queen's warrior guards was kneeling in rows in the presence of Queen Earths of Etherialah.

'From this night's moment, my soul guardians, my loyal and beloved warriors, you are to be at resting time. This is our night of celebrations for my child of countless stars. I bid you celebrate, for we have much work ahead.'

Orb had been given her seat of nurturement so that she would absorb her newly found powers. The chair had immediately become part of her being. As she watched the dance of the flowers that swayed and changed colours to the haunting music, her chair held her as a mother holding her baby.

'Mother,' she said nervously. 'My chair!'

'Shh, my daughter of my heart. All that is, is here for you. Whatever you wish, it shall be. This is sacredness itself. We are the guardians of eternities. Our very essence are the thoughts, actions and dreams of those we have charge over. It is this place of bridges that nurtures that which shall be beautiful for all realms – past, present, future – and is but the continuation of the sacredness within life forces. I am here, in this silence, when you need me. Call me within your mind. I will arrive to you, and you will know. This world is one being, where every one of us can speak to each other, connect through our thoughts and be able to protect each other whenever we wish. Our love and nurturement connect our life energies as one organism. We do not know the concepts of hate, as we have evolved from these many times through many worlds of enlightenments. But humans are now lost within their own doing; for this there is a suffering that they are imprisoned within. So, as the sands of time are running out for these beings, we must become their eyes and bring them into the Lights of Illuminations.'

'What are the Lights of Illuminations, Mother?'

'The Lights of Illuminations are our beings of sacred intentions that are born from our collective love. They themselves cannot be undone or destroyed. They are the children of us all: children that are not yet in a form that can be seen, but a form that is created from our intentional collectiveness of all that is of love. They are known as "illuminations", as this energy is something that once brought into existence will live and allow nurturement, living as the emergence of that which can never more be alone in a place of ignorances. They are the two sides of that which is and that which needs to be. The time came when we knew we had to send you across our bridge of enlightenments into that other world: the world that was formed from the wishes and endeavours of those who chose to live away from our realms. They decided they wished to live lives that could give them what they wanted, and that would create happiness. Happiness for them was to be created from what they could fashion from impermanent things: things which, if used in such a way, could give whatever they required to make them feel good. They discarded instincts, the wisdoms of sharing, compassion, integrity and nurturement, and so the innate soul began to corrupt itself. There was, and are, those who choose to cross the bridge into their sacredness, but they must battle each and every day to protect that heart of enlightenment which grows love beyond all worlds. Do you understand this, my child? Can you see what we are here to do now?'

There was a silence that stopped everything in time. No one, nothing, moved, but looked at Orb as to listen to her answer.

'I see it, Mother,' Orb replied with an expression of deep contemplation. 'I see it all, Mother. This is all in the dreams I used to have, the nightmares that would frighten me, and no one would comfort me when I was frightened. I understand now. Those, everyone else, who I felt I had no connection to, nothing in common with, as though I was a different species. So it all makes sense, when nothing before did. I understand why you could not tell of your existence. I would have been more unhappy than I was, to know that you were there, somewhere, but that I would not be able to live with you or return home. I have become stronger than I ever thought possible. To be wise yet humble is a very special thing.'

Sounds blended into beautiful scented colours, with every being in this sacred gathering dancing and holding each other's hands. Their eyes shone like lights with the purity of their love for each other. The queen had been speaking with her captain of the warriors. She then summoned over the head of horses. They smiled at each other while the captains began leading all the horses in procession back to the stables just beyond the woods. This meant that everyone was able to take up the night's celebrations. All was being taken care of. There had been much hard work of late to return Orb back home. Mead had been taken around to all the tables, with breads made from their fields of barleys. Succulent fruits, nuts and freshly gathered honey were being set out by beings called 'hummlings'. Orb was intrigued at what she believed to be humming birds. Nothing would sleep this night, as this was to be the next step in Etherialah's evolution. They had been waiting all of their lives for such a moment. The evolution of Orb.

***

The beginnings of all that was to come began that next day. Orb was up early enough to watch the sun bugs scuttling up and down the sunflowers, gathering their dewdrops for their breakfast seeds, which they made into breads that made them glow in the dark, especially when they were singing. It had started raining. The windows in Orb's bedroom trickled with raindrops that held rainbows, shimmering through the soft, pastel light sifting from the rising sun. Trees shrouded her corner garden, created for her as her little sanctuary whenever she needed a quiet place to be. The big hearth held a blazing fire; deep red embers flickered with orange snake tongues that hissed and crackled in the half-light. There was a knock on the heavy oaken door.

'Come in,' invited Orb.

'Thank you,' bowed a splendid-looking being. Her hands held a silver kindle pot for the making up of the fires. 'I am Bright Star, your personal warrior. I will be here for you, your needs, your support. I will be your mentor in all things that you wish. You may call me Star if you so wish it. My chambers have been assembled next door. Please do not hesitate to summon me at any time.'

Orb looked quizzically at Star. She was just about to say something when she heard, 'Yes! You just call me in your mind. I will hear.'

'Beautiful,' Orb replied. 'My wish then is for you to be as a friend. This is something special to me. So that we are able to be there for each other, you are now my most beloved friend forevermore.'

Bright Star began to cry with happiness and ran to Orb with the biggest, warmest hug in the universe. 'I would so love to be your friend, to be here for you whenever needed, and you for me. Thank you with all my heart, Orb, forever.'

That day, when all was as should be for Orb's homecoming, the evening had been arranged for Orb to join everyone within Etherialah's realm that were off duty, apart from the imperial guards of warriors; these were chosen for overseeing protection of the gatekeepers. Their resting time would be at the end of the week's celebrations of return. Orb's mother and father spoke with her to explain that there was to be this time to meet all, to be at one with her new realms of nurturement.

A moment came that evening when Orb met Moon Swordmaker, the captain of the highest guards. The captains were as female and male, so that both sides of the balance of sacredness would grow in harmony. Moon Swordmaker was the son of the high captain of warrior guards.

From this moment of meeting, for Orb, Moon Swordmaker would be forever her completeness. In the course of time, they would be Etherialah's strengthening. Their unity as one was to grow and nurture all that their world would create with their beauty of souls. Here our world awaits. Silently within dreams we await. There we shall awake consciousness. We are the awakening.

***

All Will Come

There is a place where light enters,
Where innocence dwells within Orbs of enlightenment.
It will grow from sacredness that breathes within;
You just need to be that silence.

Where we are awaits,
For this change has come in all we are.
I am voices of eternal spirit,
Guiding those lost amid life's storms.

I am this shield to hold tears of your compassions,
With all you are be mighty.
Warrior within your realms to protect,
Be more than blood and bone upon this earth.
Then all you shall be
Will be others' guides of light,
To bring perpetual effects.

This place where you cannot see
Has waited vast and many lifetimes,
For those who live in despair
May now arrive and cross their bridge of hopes.

Though wisdom is a door of possibilities;
It bears no key which you may find.
Impassable labyrinths unfurl throughout all journeys,
Here in your mind of shadows.
Are destinations to give you sanctuaries?
Protect your soul with love that bless and bind.

Where then is your road of endless journeys?
Is it where your heart beats now?
If not, find yourself amid destructive spectres,
And pray that you can allow;
Allow peace to enter the beating of your heart;
Allow that which you have stopped
To breathe again and start.

You have more than you can see:
Time to look deeper,
Time to set yourself free.
In this doing, you will understand
What then you have within your hands.

Here, at this place in time,
You are everything you could wish to be.
May you live for that love created, now and evermore,
In the universe of our creation.

We must shine for to light our way.
We are that which gives life to our love in all its forms.
We possess our own skies in which to fly.
We are that nurturement within the seeds of life.

So there is a key which you must fashion
From the grains of your sacred soul;
One which cannot be lost or forsaken.
Its metal is of your wisdom that is forged by your love.
It is all to give, and so you shall reap all that you shall sow.

Love is the bridge to all eternities,
Built from dreams of the stars inside our minds.
With strength and the will to give,
It will hold all your love that you care to carry.

With each step there is loving;
By your strength it will find.
All that is waiting will be inside your heart;
Beauty to make your home forever inside.

Life is that which you are bestowed.
While you may be with all that you wish,
There is a place where nothing but love can adorn you.
Open your heart; there is no time to resist.

Softly, let your thoughts fly free,
Into the skies of truth and tranquillities.
Far from all desires awaits peace of the heart.
Freedom awaits in your hopes;
Freedom is given in the solace of your dreams.

Step forth across your bridge.
It will take you where you need to be.
Enter its new lands of nurturement.
Here, where the light from your healing can see.

If you follow your heart,
It will find many places you have never known;
But know now you are that seed of life.
This new world is listening for your footsteps
Upon its earth,
Within this soul.

To let go of those things that obscure your light,
To breathe deeply this magnificence of being,
To stand with warriors, infinite and immortal,
Your bridge is your love.
Follow your path of truths;
See, and your instincts will uncover.

When confusions carried your heart
To those fears from hell and heartaches,
Pain was that sanctuary that only wounded.
To begin that journey to your place of knowing
Is to be fearless amid many demons;
And to share that light from your darkest fears
Is to plant countless trees and help them grow.
We are those who give of our love.
We are given its sacredness of knowledge.

Humilities

Where you can walk in those places of imbalance,
Walk there with humilities.
When you can guide any soul who has lost their way,
Whisper kind words without judgements.

If you are hurting from your own wounds,
Hold out your hands.
You will know what is needed.
Be silence.
Be those senses that will show how to heal.

Can you give all your love
To that soul who has nothing?
From the most fragile corners of your mind,
Could you reach out your hands and cradle theirs?

How would it be to understand that which you do not
possess?
Would you know how to nurture without trust?
This may be more than you would allow.
Who then bears this cost of such pain?

So when the battle is lost, though many won,
Call your heavens that they may shield,
With mightiest of wings to hold your heart.

It is the call of warriors
That will lead you through your labyrinths.
Fears do not steal their might.
Fear not;
They wait for your return,
To carry in this light.
Now will you be that saving grace,
Full with giving and that which loves?

Then we shall be that everything
That grows with beauty.
In cold abandonments you will be that warmth,
When those so lost can return home.

Our Legacies

I have wished to count the stars,
And they have proved impossible.
I have seen this world in suffering,
And she calls out to all of us.
I heed her cries with all I am,
So this soul shall find all of the pieces
Lost along our corridors of abandonments.

I have felt mankind's cruel heart,
And our ears do become unhearing.
I have watched beyond all endurance,
But now discovered,
And so freed myself from that fearing.

I have travelled through many worlds that are beyond our
    comprehensions,
And we have incredible things to learn.
I have talked with those of ancient tongues,
And now I speak.

To be loved is where all things are possible.
This law is one of infinite times.
There is nothing that cannot be created sacred.
To be loved are all things impossible;
To be loved is where earth meets our skies;
To be loved, we are all that is beautiful.
In fire, earth, water and winds
We are the coming of our breath.

To be loved when love has been torn away;
To be loved within the ticking of our days;
To be loved as one who is your heartbeat;
To be loved in that moment of your meeting.

It is all.
It is silence on a mountain;
It is forest upon rich earth;
It is oceans of deep longings;
It is giving amid loss.
It is growing beneath desolations;
It is abundance within loss;
It is companionship after abandonments;
It is fire within indifference.
It is solace from tides of fears;
It is a unique journey with a friend;
It is humility of wisdoms;
It is voices spoken where no one dwells;
It is shelter when you are lost;

It is food shared from poverty;
It is companionship found from loneliness;
It is forgiveness forged into understandings;
It is a child nurtured without selfishness;
It is life breathed into the resurrected;
It is my soul's sacredness become eternities;
It is love.

This Journey

While living is the journey we are taken upon,
There can be many journeys that we must follow.
Some may show us how we need to live;
Some may lead us into fearful worlds,
May dismantle strengths and soul.

By our hands we can build such might and majesties;
Of our hearts we have such strengths.
With compassions all moves towards this light;
And with love illuminate our worlds.

Create from your mind's imagination.
Speak from your heart; it has many voices.
Understand with your eyes; they interpret all language.
Listen with your instincts; they are your immortal voice.

Within those shadows of doubts,
There dwells seeds of your possibilities.
Upon the highest point of insecurities,
Stand upon your own place of strengths.
Break free chains of fear and fearsome torments.

This day we have that chance;
Chance bestowed once, then once now.
This day we have new journeys.
For all they were,
For all they are,
For all they will be,
We are overflowing with abundance.

Shall then you hide inside your broken dreams?
Should then your life be as an abandoned child?
Lift all veils upon your sight.
Here we may venture throughout our paradise,
To follow paths that call us.

We are as sunshine that warms this earth;
We are that insurmountable place;
We are that ship on this sea of life.
Together we are community;
Together we are that place that's home.

Travel where you can find the lost.
Keep safe your gifts of kindness and compassions.
Share all you are with those wounded along your way.
Enlighten with each grain of love.
Be that which is strength
For those who have lost more than they can bear,
For those who have nothing left to say.

I Am Strength

A moment of time can change our very souls;
Small is this journey of time.
Yet, for all our endeavours there is one point of light
We cannot reach as yet.
Here it lives from all our choices,
All our deeds;
It lives among our most forgotten dreams.

While your life awaits its purpose,
Show me where you are.
So many stumble in their ignorance.
Let us help light their way.

Come take my hand;
There is nothing to fear.
Come take my hand;
I see our way,
I am Here.

Find me; I am your sanctuary.
When you have given all you are,
I will hear your cries.
Find me; I am your warrior,
In life and beyond all deaths.
I live eternal,
To take you home.

Come take my hand;
You have nothing to fear.
Come take my hand;
I am Here.

When your mind can feel no peace,
You shall be contentment.
Come take my hand;
I will always be here.

When you are weary
From so much of life's heartaches,
Come take my hand;
I will give you my strengths.

You are love that comes from innocence.
You are that love unending.
You are the oasis found in the desert.
You are the return of all that has been lost.
You are where healing begins.

Sphere of Resurrection

The emergence of all that is beautiful;
A completeness of a knowing of something more than us.
Love is everything you do not own;
It is the abundance of that which relates with all.
Love is our convergence.

Love is the birthing of all that is;
A dance of universal sacredness.
Something more than us.

Love creates everything you do not possess.
It is abundance of that which connects with all.
Love is infinite by its own powers.

Love is the soul of all that is;
A breath of that which needs no form.
Love reveals deceits and destructions;
It is unceasing from that which is one with all.
Love is everlasting: has no beginnings, needs no ends.

Love is the all,
The mind which speaks to us without voice.
In that something where our senses dwell,
Love is neither here nor there.
Love grows from hopes weaved into a broken soul;
Love feeds a starving spirit;
Love builds from the hurts of a broken heart.

It is this substance of love,
Its formulations that we may be blessed enough to absorb.
I stand as warrior to carry all that must be,
For within this incandescence of such magic
I hold this sacredness with all I am.

As Love protects this gate I keep,
So there to open without falsehoods,
I hold this sacredness with all I am,
To guide that way upon those I love.

Innocence

Children are brought from magical worlds;
They are our teachers.
Child is a spirit of infinite innocence;
They have gentilities that must be protected.
Within them is a place where they see much more.

Pain can be that place where the child has no choices.
Where there is no choice, there is a suffering.
Suffering creates destructions of oneself
And the dreams of possibilities.

Child is a vessel for allowance.
Allow this to shed its light.
As warrior I protect innocence.
It is all and more than I am.

If your wisdom has grown,
The child will be that seed of nurturement,
Nurturement that you have grown.
You will have created that which nothing can destroy.
It is then that all shall be understood.

As you walk with humilities and understandings,
Lift your eyes above.
You will live with knowledge that has no bounds;
That point of omnipotence, where earth meets our heavens.
We are the keepers of that sacredness.
It is we who must learn to become child.

Child within us,
See our souls within your eyes.
It is here that is lost amid our greed,
As you grow towards your sky.
Open your hearts inside your world of being.
Forgive us for our ignorance and shallow needs.

Grow each seed with time.
Grow each seed with gentleness.
Grow each seed with happiness.
Grow each seed with love.

ur Return

Far from this world there live fantastical things;
Do you wish to follow me?
Here in this world live fantastical things;
Can you not awake to see?

For all you find along your way, be humble;
We do not know upon which fateful day we shall fall.
If then our journeys have led us to stumble,
We only need to hold out our hand and call.

We do not need to fear anything but ignorance;
Our strengths can tear apart such ill-made walls.

All roads lead back home;
This realm is just a moment in which to grow.
So when you understand this reason for this life,
You will have travelled far.

By knowing where you must venture,
You can guide those who have stumbled along the way.
Trust in all you have become, my friend,
As you return home again
To nurture,
To grow,
To love,
To know.
You can never be anywhere but home.

Understanding now where you must venture,
You will guide those who have stumbled along their way.
There, trust in all that you have fought to become,
When time for you to return home again.
Now you can nurture.
Now you do grow.
Now you are love.
Sacredness abides within your heart.
You are nevermore to be far from home.

Miracles

Slow motion,
Visions in violet,
Stealth without labour,
Mercurial magnificence,
Fierce animation,
Energised urgencies in movements,
Silence suspended,
Surreal splendour,
Iridescence of illusions of mind,
Expanse of ether expressions paused,
Reflective resurrections,
Nature's laws,
Feathered guardians of futures,
Feathered warriors of sacredness,
Incomprehensible reverence,
Humility of heart,
Intelligence insurmountable,
Wisdom of a higher order,
Kaleidoscopic symmetries convergence.

As we are bound to this earth,
You are as breeze upon our skies.
Best there we look towards our stars,
To gather in this glimpse of miracles.

Peace

And while there is a space for us to breathe,
Allow it too for sacredness.
In solitude and silence, it shall always be.
Mind, spirit and soul that owns eternities.

While all we do has meaning,
Listen inside our beating truth of hearts.
Then so be it those who lose the light of immaculate.
Cry not for self-loss when stumbled inside your
    abandonment.

For there the grace,
For there the mighty.
For there the strength of the naive.
For there the love,
For there the selflessness.
For there the passion,
For there lies endless compassion.

While there is time that is given,
It is allotted for a reason.
In understanding, we need no fears,
For peace is ours for all seasons.

To find peace when only fears remain;
To find peace when life has filled with pain;
To find peace when there is no one by your side;
To find peace when kindness has all but died.

Then be that silence in your scream;
Then be that calm within your storm;
Then be that fire to cleanse your wounds;
Then be that journey when you are lost and worn.

Here dwell hearts of a thousand warriors,
Amid thunderous waves upon mighty rock.
You walk as silence upon thought.
It is I who are without you by my side,
Dissolved within our longings,
As foam upon a distant shore.

I send you my dreams on oceans of stars,
That you will see them before they melt across the morning
    skies.
I walk softly upon the echoes of your heart.
Until then we walk together;
Until then we talk together.
And here is my soul.

There I see you walk far away from where I am;
But all the seconds of our fleeting time,
I walk with you through these different lands.
Mere time cannot erase one grain of all we are.
I too dream your dreams with all I am.

I shall be waiting to catch your hand again.
There is no fearing from my heart,
As this Love can only grow stronger.
You will hear me in your sunshine and in your shadows.
I am here to walk with you for all times.

Abundance

Earth aches through blood-red stars.
So small are we that wield powers beyond imagination;
And yet we have much to learn.
If we begin now, we will find the way.

Our dreams are that we learn to share,
But greed is ours to gain without care.
Yet we have endless, more than heavens count our infinite stars,
To climb stairs of inspirations,
And walk into the skies,
To dream of what we can achieve
From working for the good of everything.

If we pick up all our pieces together,
We can create more than we could ever know.
Be humility in your arrogance;
Be giving in your lacking;
Be loving in your selfishness;
Be abundance in all emptiness.

Child of Stars

Child of stars, sleep now,
For tonight you can be everything you can dream.
And dance with angels on splendid clouds,
When morning comes.
Tell me, if you wish,
Where you have been.

I hold you tight
With all my might.
I will fill your heart with happiness and love.
So always know that no matter where you go,
I am with you in your dreams.

Child of stars, sleep tight now,
For you are my beautiful shining light.
So fill those stars with all your love.
When morning comes,
Tell me, if you wish,
Where you planted all your dreams.

I hold you tight,
With all my might.
You fill my heart with happiness and love.
Just always be that gentle child.
There you will be with me in my dreams.

In times ahead you will learn so much,
So many wonderful things to behold.
Always come home to me.
Home is where I shall always be.

Child of stars,
Shine brighter than you have shone before.
I will carry you through your nightmares.
I will laugh with you in your dreams.

Here in my arms, so sleep now.
There is always our love that will keep us strong.
When you hear me call, when you feel alone,
Here I will be to carry you home.

In good times and in sad,
Here is where we can create new journeys.
So grow now, my beloved child,
And we will learn to nurture and grow.

When others have lost their way,
We shall arrive home together for tea;
And there talk into the night
Of how to fill our days with love.

We hide ourselves behind so many masks,
Abiding in our hidden places
Without fate nor favour,
Nor thought for tomorrow's seeds to grow into wisdoms.

Call me, then,
For I have seen this spectre,
Too dreadful to behold.
So see all that is silence,
Be all that is silence,
Feel all that is silence.
With your instincts,
Be that strength of conscience.

Embrace love with a thousand longings;
Be that drummer in an empty heart.
Find the shadows within the light;
Understand all endings before you start.

The gate of our undoings stands strong;
Behind lies the key to where we belong.
It is on the other side of this gate,
The key that defines illusions,
Where we choose to look,
But refuse to see.

Past has come to teach the present.
As for our future?
It waits.
And as it waits, our time running to meet our future,
So fast it is with wings.

Watch what you create.
Make them with all the love you are.
From where you learn how sacred life is,
Is when you have nothing but beauty to give.

Child of stars, shine for me
With your endless love,
Inside your beauteous light.
Child of stars, shine bright for me.
I shall dwell within your dreams tonight.

Child of stars, shine for me,
With eyes filled with endless love.
Child of stars, shine bright for me;
I am here forevermore.

Our Captain Tom

Born to be remembered far beyond this life,
A warrior throughout history.
Strength of many thousand armies,
You gave of yourself so selflessly.

When time came to stand at ease,
You gave more than one man would give.
Captain Tom, you have shown us how we need to live.
You taught us how we must learn to give of ourselves.

We know not what each day will give,
But our purpose is to work as one.
With fragile steps and mighty mind,
You had no fears of failing.

Now our lives will 'best be good'!
Our warrior that lived 'this sunny day'!

Here our lives shall be incredible,
As you would always remind us
In your humble, humorous way.
We all can still hear the words you did say,
No matter what,
Our tomorrows shall be 'a good day'!

Thank you, Captain Tom;
You showed us how to live.
In the midst of sadness and sufferings,
You gave all that you could give.

And while the time has passed along,
Your legacy of compassion still lives on.
There is nothing so great as to be grateful.
Be that strength.
Be that humility.
When all is lost,
Be that light.

Our Captain Tom, you lived your best.
You are a legend we can all learn to be.
Now in our hearts you have left your dreams.
Throughout each day,
We too will know just what it takes to care,
Just why we need to share.
In living our today,
As one family we can make that difference universally.

Breathe Now

Breathe now;
You are safe from injustice and brutality.
Breathe now;
The world watched you die.

I am so sorry for this price you had to pay,
By those who could not understand.
Our hearts are heavy with this weight of pain,
But that door to enlightenment has been torn down.

Breathe now, George Floyd;
We never knew your name before.
Angels protect your soul forevermore.
Though we can never forget,
We know this moment has changed complacency.

Cry we must,
With tears to heal our world,
For you walk now within our history,
In safekeeping for those to come.
Time has come.
Our race is one;
Our race is human;
Our fate is in our hands.

That road to freedom has been so hard to find.
So long;
So long walking.
When all those words were spoken,
With humility they sang.
Even though their hearts were broken.

Breathe now, gentle Perry.
Your life has and always shall be
Our light to guide us homewards,
Here to live in peace and togetherness.
To be all that is incredible,
And be those guardians of this world's communities.
Now we must give back with gratitude and humilities;
For without, these graces are our road to wisdom.

There can be no forgetting your sacrifice;
I will always be grateful to have known you.
Only a fleeting moment in our consciousness,
Forever will you live within our memories.
You showed us all how ignorance is a mask

That allowed to fall can show how grotesque we choose to
    be.

BEHIND THE MASKS

Morning had opened its heavy eyes upon our stone-grey street. It stared upon the tumble toss of red-bricked terraced houses, peering through the transparency of timbered windows, pipped privets tucked in some of the odd-shaped, emerald-green gardens. Arty coloured flowers clustered here and there, snuggled into crevices and cracks to create homes, and comfy ones at that, for all manner of little flitter-bugs that always have important work to do for our planet. Today was Friday. That said, Friday is a sneaky imposter at pretending to be a day where you can ease back the gears, just a bit. Most Fridays I have frequented have been the most fast-forwarded and frantic days of my entire hectic life.

Neighbours appeared as if birthed from various front doors along pale pavements that held all our working-class houses together. Mrs O'Shay, shuffling gingerly from her corner shop, trying her best not to go faster than her worn-out legs would carry her. Heaven help her if she came across an object at speed. There would be nothing left, I suspect. Maybe a shredded pile of clothes and a stubborn, old cardigan that matched her nature. She ran our community corner shop. I seemed to visit like a second home. It just sold anything that she could get hold of at the time. If you asked, she would order things in and then start selling that item from then on. Many things were still in the original box; it was all too much to unpack everything when they were going to be taken out then sold anyway. I was with her 100 per cent on that, as things in boxes always possessed an intrigue and that touch of mystery I have never grown out of. An emporium of endless odds and ends that seemed to include everything that every other shop on the street sold, except

Mrs O'Shay's were special. She stocked everything around her collection of hard-boiled sweets, layers of big glass jars alive with colours. At some point it was obvious she was not able to reach the majority of jars, so she would shout at the side door behind the counter, and in would stride her son, who, through my eyes, was around eight feet tall.

I needed to be around genuine people today, if any people at all. Sociability I now understood was a trait you either possessed or made by choice. From an early age I discovered that for me it was most definitely not the former. Never could behave quite as others in my peer group. Creativity was definitely my bag: had it in sackloads. Once school began, playing had a compartmental feel about it. Different. Set times, order and routine that took you by surprise at the start then became your normal routine that was anything but normal to me. Outside the windows was where I understood my world resumed, where I knew everything worth knowing in my world, as small as it was. To the naked eye my little world was no bigger than an eye of an extremely miniature needle. But to me, and I knew what I knew, my world was bigger than the brief history of time—my time. Dislodging the vivid events of my first day of school always reinforces my sense of unusualness. Upon arriving with Mother firmly cemented to my right hand, I knew life for me had slid into an abyss of fear and foreboding. All I had ever known up to that point was chaos and chances to escape into my fantasy realm of freedom and fun and that essential ingredient any hyperactive child must contain: imagination dipped in defiance.

Within the first few, thankfully short, hours, I was gone! I had come up with the rouse of 'Toilet, please'. I retraced the cloakroom, which happened to be the vestibule for the toilets as well, realising the side exit was there! Without glancing back I was out, heading west towards home.

Resuming my past events of that day, I am more than certain I would have been able to find my way home across a continent with the amount of determination stored within my spritely body. At that moment there was no tethering me to anything that resembled normality.

But I knew soon I would have to dance to their unending tunes in order to force myself into the rigidities of humanity's treadmills. I believe that to this day I have not recovered from this psychological assault. Throughout the torturous hours ahead, where I was subjected to simultaneous interrogations by both my mother and the school truancy detective, I learnt how all-encompassing parental powers really are. Next day I would be escorted, albeit under duress, by Mother and the grip of death. She was not letting go of me, even if it meant her battling a hoard of ninjas.

***

I soon discovered my new red wool, double-breasted, full-length winter coat was gone! For some reason I believed school was a place where things stayed, like it was too important a place for anyone to steal anything from. I went to the local museum for the first time, and I remember that feeling. If you stole anything from such places, you would be taken away by people in suits and removed from the planet.

'Just great!' I heard myself say. Something else to pile onto the mound of grievances that waited for me, like the biggest book in the world catalogued with my perpetual defiances.

Home was not a destination I chose as first choice; home was a place of pain and punishment for this little bod. My number one mind and body sanctuary was the hill. I lived at the base of the mother of all hills. Although it is called a hill, to all intents and purposes it is a mountain. Most of the streets on my block rose upwards towards the hill. It was a steep incline, quite deceptive to anyone on a basic shuffle-about mode. Exploring my neighbourhood would teach me more than any schooling could by a manic mile. Living with grown-ups, no matter who they are, is an endless journey through the twilight zone, and there are no guarantees of any exits.

Children are immensely strong. The abilities required to learn, adapt and evolve are incredibilities I am fascinated by. When abandoned by all that is nurturing, children—some more than others—can and will overcome, thrive and, if all their stars are in alignment, evolve in such a way as to be mentors of the highest calibre to those in most need of rescuing from their fate worse than destruction.

So, with such poverty-stricken odds, how would this be possible? Looking through my odd-shaped window as a child, understanding as many pieces of my jigsaw as I have battled to gain parts of, there is a jewel of wisdom stored away in the deepest recesses of those few children who can and will be activated in the event of abandonment on any level. Humilities are formed by the sheer love and determination of that particular individual, a strength of character that is visible to the naked eye. Silent acknowledgement of others' pain and persecutions, with the untouchable senses that will connect and comfort in such a way as to be unnoticed but leave an indelible mark of nurturement on those it connects with.

As for growing up, it happened to me. Never seemed to live it as if I was part of the accumulations of days, months, years that fell into an entanglement of peoples, times, things that created and controlled other things that made up life. Being different had its advantages in a strange sort of way.

An only child, with a mother who had no clue how to bring up a child with love and integrity—outside events were of more importance than a little bundle of innocence and dependency.

So in the event of indifference, break glass; be a self-contained unit; look for the cracks in the walls of supposed securities; grow your own planet of survival in the midst of an apocalypse; plant good strong seeds in your postage-sized garden; save your compost for recycling all those grotty, used and abused dregs of experiences and treat them as if they were gems found along your cheap and cheerful patch of nurturement, where the best of the day's sun chooses to shine on each seedling needing the best start for its nurturing life to come. The end of one day has filled your heart with so much happiness, that there's half a barrowload waiting for your next.

Something I found on an extraordinarily regular basis was unusualness: things that invariably led to people who turned out to be different. That very fact for me was, and is, the most fabulous honour. I built me my own little sanctuary. Something to read up in the book of 'how to live and survive the journey' is how to learn to change your nature to your best advantage. Nature for me is an abundance of beautiful sacredness. I had then, as I have now, a presence of being that would only give of its best. That is how it was, how it always shall be.

***

Finding a first job from school carries with it an excitement. Becoming part of something so huge as society was somewhere too scary to even contemplate. To obtain a job was to be a viable human in my observant eyes. That sound of 'When can you start?' was to be Sherlock Holmes waiting on an intriguing case that would turn out to be *The Hound of the Baskervilles*. Whatever was available that was an ordinary, normal job was one I would take. There can be no book about growing up that would do justice to those of us who believe they are not as everyone else. Everyone else has some sort of choice they can assert in their growing-up lives. Never be afraid to be unusual. Being yourself is a truly special way of being. To be a loving, nurturing soul is the stuff dreams are made of – literally! Whatever age you are, or wish to be, is how it should be. Our gifts of life are the most magical and mysterious experiences being alive has bestowed upon us.

We have no concept of this experience we are now part of. Do we know where we wish to be? What we wish to be part of? Who we wish to create, or who we are? Presumptuous or not, I don't believe we do. This mind-blowing mystery tour of life is made up of so many more manifestations of possibilities, that we are completely overwhelmed by the data, the invisibilities of configurations, re-animations and alternate communications flung across our fragile interpretations. We are, to a greater extent, passengers that have been issued a ticket to destinations unknown. From my starting block, I carried a heavy burden of responsibilities. To be adopted at the get-go, but to be allowed those occasional off-leash hours where you returned back to base more traumatised than when you left. That raw longing for the father you are not allowed to live with, grow up around, learn from, absorb wisdom from or nurture his individualities within yours.

And the child I was reconfigured the conflicting information. Adaptation was, it seems, a dominant skill. For, after all of that which should have irreparably damaged such a genteel psyche, I survived. Not just survived, but grew with powerful strength of character, with a rare ability to be something most different, that matters in this unchartered space called Earth. Everything must matter here, where we, as a race, wield so much power, along with an insatiable appetite for self-survival at most cost. Children can adapt in hostile environments as nature's diversity must day in, day out. When my day-to-day life changed its circumstances, *I* changed *me*, so that I could still take care of those responsibilities more heavily bestowed upon me and absorb the damage. So many jobs, so much damage on all levels, so much adaptation. Some for the better, some …? Maybe it is time that will adapt any negative elements and turn them into far more than positive. Something other-worldly I feel is the alchemist. All that base, raw life is necessary to make the highest grade preciousness.

Whenever the time arrives when this child can put down that weapon of an unnatural responsibility, that calm will be there waiting. A place to rest. A place to grow. A place to evolve.

In that final analysis I do believe that wealth is a vehicle capable of creating fantastical innovations that will elevate cause and communities: that it is not the wealth that holds the key, but the machine of humanity that is constructed to work together to achieve the total support needed by and for this planet. It is *us* who are the wealth, *us* who are the force of energies required to fuel and animate this inanimate construct that we have allowed to submerge our consciousness under the weight of its shiny facades.

Whenever you wish to return to who you are, go sit in your garden for a while. Just be still. Just listen with your eyes. See with your mind. Become that moment without thoughts. Allow yourself to become that silence and to find that thread of sacredness that will connect all that you are.

Home Is Where You Both Are

Walk, little child;
I have come to take you home.
Lift up your sleepy head,
And I will carry you.

Sing, little child;
I have heard you in my heart.
Show me how happy you are,
And I will know peace.

Be all that you are, little child,
Fears have no place in your worlds.
Just live from your love,
And I will grow towards the sky.

Laugh through your pains, little child;
Good things will always keep you safe.
You are born to light lost paths;
All is here in safekeeping.

This journey is ours together,
It was always meant to be.
Growing through all these lonely worlds,
With no one to guide our ways.
Look! We have made it all with love,
And wisdom of how to live each day.

Sleep now, little child;
You have worked so hard.
Tomorrow has many things for your nurture,
So I will carry you home.

When time has grown you,
We are as one.
Where only love is all we need,
Here is our sacred place;
Our home where we shall be.
Together now,
Together then.
Here we can find all of our dreams.

Sleep now, little child;
You have worked so hard.
Tomorrow has many things for you to nurture.
You have given so much beauty in this world today;
Now I am here to carry you home.

FINDING A WAY HOME

Bridges are those which carry us from one world into another. They allow us opportunities to change perspective. Your bridge can open a door to possibilities you would only dream of.

Mothers who would give more of themselves than they have been given are those miracles in life that can go unnoticed. I see you.

There I see her, lost in her lonely, abandoned world of struggle. No more than slight, but with the indelible strength only found in few. Hurting from the wound of leaving her home, all she knew. And now there was no one. Father had passed from over-work and lack of love. Everything that held all those self-sustaining structures necessary to build you into a balanced individual had been eroded away through deliberate, destructive manipulation of innocence and incredibly unrelenting jealousies. Selfishness too easily applied, while in the guise of a mother. The fact was, my worth lies in being a powerful pawn in the ugly game of parental chess. My father loved me more than his own life, but love can be a cruel overseer too. To keep me in his life as safely as possible meant I had to have a mother. This woman, hardly known, with highly efficient survival skills, would be at that right place for my time. But she knows that she is only existing. Another low-paid job? Another relocation by her mother, so as not to grow roots and live her happy life, free? At the first sign of someone getting too close, she would have to be uprooted into another area, or city. She was her adoptive mother's meal ticket from Dad's loyal support machine. There was no way they could live together without killing each other on some level. Solutions?

Different cities. Physically far enough, but close enough to allow for financial chains to both feed the famine and fuel the fires. She went home so tired from menial work. This was everything she had ever known. This would be good enough for her, because looking after her father's choice of a mother was to repay with my heart and soul.

Not for so long, though, she felt happy. Someone seemed to care something for her, and that was just fine. Within a short time the man whom she had decided to make her best friend there on her night shift had filled that painful wound with each meet. She had found a source of contentment to try to heal.

Throughout each hateful conflict with her mother, she grew too weakened to allow another piece of herself to be dismantled. Time had come to leave this endless battle that gave permission to destroy her selfless love, and she accepted that she wished to cross the bridge. The man she made her friend, maybe he would have the love that she had always had. Maybe she could grow her beauty with that soulmate she had lost in her father. So much love she had to give, to grow all that indestructible nurturement within her children to come. Here were all of her dreams, the longings that one day she would be that devoted, enduring and evolving mother she was never to be blessed with herself.

***

It was around three years, by moving in together, that they became closer, doing those things that looked after each other and making a home together. Her mother had realised that she had lost the most incredible, loving and most selfless companionship she would know in all worlds. It had come time for that miracle to enter Little Mother's most loving world. For her, she felt free for the first time. Her belief was that from hereon in her life would blossom into a fabulous world of love and creativity.

In the course of a few short years together, then getting married, her first baby girl was born. Her wish was that she would have two little girls. They would grow up together, nurturing each other to be the incredible individuals they were meant to be.

These souls would be bestowed with something indelible that would never be lost, abused or abandoned, ever. With the growing of these lives, she also grew in ways never imagined.

***

To talk was to understand that speaking. She would be speaking for her daughters when they could not. To feel, with the knowledge that feelings were to be of the best, the strongest, the most loving, the most creative. And these girls would know such love and devotion, that they would physically feel it within every movement and glance.

As always, too much hard work was the shackles that kept mother-to-be trapped by her own depth of nurturing nature that was the air she breathed, all she had ever known.

There was no other family to confide in or console with when times were at their worst. Along her way she found some lifelong friends who were always there, waiting and supporting her in fabulous and fine ways. Asking for help was never who she was though. Life had taught her many things; being dependent on anyone was not one of them. These friends, who either came and went or became her life companions, taught her endless things that made everything good and gave her strength to be there for those she loved.

Her baby girls created completeness, connected to the child within herself. Her senses were heightened for this, the biggest challenge in her challenging life.

When her daughters were around three and five she realised this partnership she was working so hard to bring into the positive light, so that working hard together would ensure her girls' happy and healthy childhoods. As months turned into three gruelling and extremely fearful years, she could not gloss over the cracks any more. Children, as is known, see the truth behind the mask. To stay would be to live without integrities, that distinction between that which determines how we should live, not how to pretend to exist.

The choice would be to leave with no means of support, only little cleaning jobs that demanded every ounce of energy for the lowest pay. With lack of finances came lack of support on all levels of existence. The house that was to grow her babies and family would need to be sold and they would now have to rent. Within the course of a few short months, they had a rental house. From beginnings, she gave it her all. Whatever it took, she would give. Charity shops, the first port of call for this, that and something for tomorrows. The girls loved the terraced house. Old, Victorian, high ceilings, and windows that let in the best of light. A little back yard that had traces of something grander in its heydays. We ate at the kitchen table that fitted nicely into the middle room that held on to the tiny kitchen that was an add-on somewhere along its path of history.

There it was again. That day crept in without her noticing. They had to leave this home too. School nursery day. The sky had decided to unleash torrents of sheer water from its slate-grey ocean above us. The journey was something that could be a happy adventure for her girls since her eldest had begun. The day of days would be that day to remember forever. The car would not be travelling anywhere. As the rain poured, she looked out, readied for their school journey, macs and wellies fitted with little beautiful faces that filled with tears when told we had to walk. Smallest first, whisked up into her busy arms, then her hand took hold of her eldest. School would be a journey of change for the three of them. Upon arrival she handed over her girls. They were soaked to the bone. So was she, but it did not matter; her babies were in safely and would be dry and warmed by their nurturing teachers.

The local newsagent's held the newspaper that would give her hope for a home, just for the babies and her. She had enough for a certain paper that held the rentals for the areas she needed, to be able to ensure that her girls could stay in their lovely, original, old school she instinctively knew would be a good force for the beginnings of their great journeys ahead. She would make certain of that. One advert had been made for her needs. She rang the number. A soft, intelligent voice replied. By the end of the conversation she was offered the flat. But, as nervously repeated, she had no finances. The lovely lady told her that she would let her the flat, as she had a good feeling about this moment. 'Please don't worry about anything. We will make this happen!' So this moment happened. Two little innocents, with well-used wellies, were to have a home. Their mother had moved heaven and earth to ensure this would be that moment of miracles, that she had found that bridge. Next step would be to allow that strength to breathe, so that they three could have a home to grow together.

Packing most essentials was packing away that place called home and family. This was for her to take over everything that was and is, where her true being lives.

That flat became the home where they could feel loved without fearing that one day all would be taken from them and life would be upended again. It is incredible how resilient a child is in the midst of turbulent and terrible ways of living; how their hearts can be broken into many pieces, but then have the magnificence to mend them back together.

So with every day, the pages turned for this little family of females. A nurturing, loving mother, as is a father, has the capacity to be both sides of a child's universe if so required.

I know this beautiful mother to this day. She is, and will forever be, in my life. Her journey has been something so magical, so indelible, so evolving that I now understand that anything is possible if you so wish it. She is a warrior. I believe from her first point of arrival upon this planet, she would be a piece of star that could, and would, rise to those impossibilities that held something without name, something ancient—an incandescence that if overcome would have all power to instigate great change: change of our status quo, change of our poisoned roots of indifferences, greed and nurturement of all that is inhuman. The mother who knows no limitations of her abundance of love will create a constant perpetuation of rejuvenation in all things. Her love is our original core of what we are here for, stripped bare of deceptions and demons. In among us all there is a bridge that we are able to cross so that we may discover our own truths, our own limitless potentials.

Finding your strength upon your life's journey is not for the faint-hearted. Whether you wish to be someone who lives life only for yourself, or whether your life is for being that bridge so that others can find their way also, this journey is our most incredible and incomprehensible one. It most certainly requires your complete integrity. It must have your selfless participation. As you journey through whatever landscapes come your way though, be that being which, no matter what, gives of the most beautiful best of yourself, because in this final analysis we have been allowed this life so that we may, in turn, nurture all that is life. Life is that dream we can only create together.

Something else …

Orb, her beautiful two daughters and wonderful partner in life grew together. Their daughters were known as The Orblings. Living was loving and nurturing all life within their realms. Life as they had been taught is a journey that we have the power to charter.

The storms will always find us, but our will shall always return us home.

ORBLINGS OF ILLUMINATIONS I

On this day The Orblings discovered much destruction within the most fabulous forest they had seen upon this earth. Man had taken so much of that which was of nature itself. Skies had grown dark with a heavy sorrow of lost, lonely and wounded beings that are our earth's sacred sentient beings. No one seemed to care. All that was left was a world of selfishness and ignorance. This world of man was a manifestation of all the destructions of those beautiful dreams that we as humans can create with our abilities of communication.

As The Orblings had been born with the art of signing, they spoke to each other in their silent dance. This was one of their ways of communication with all sentient beings Over much time those beings explained that through many years they had suffered in so many ways. Much of their world was destroyed; much was changed in such a way as to never be able to sustain their lives again. Mothers with their babies, so beautiful, so unique, told their stories with tears in their eyes, holding each other tight. The fathers who were still alive spoke of days and nights that would take away fantastical swathes of forests and pollute crystal-clear rivers far into the distance. All beauty that is their world's would be as man's insatiable thirst for wealth that would not be quenched. So living for them was now the darkest battle for survival. Those who could take their families and hide somewhere else may have survived, only for others never to be seen again. And so, forest and all that is earth's sacredness itself was left bereft of its heart and soul, lost and abandoned to the cruelties of humanity. Earth's point of light was growing dim. Those humans who would not listen to the beauty of their hearts had chosen to destroy that which nurtures all. As they became without connection to their own beauty, they themselves lost the instincts of all natural senses that all beings are given.

Upon learning all this pain, The Orblings cried bitter tears with all that was there. From then on they knew humanity had lost its way. Working together with one nurturing mind is your only chance of life, for all they told those humans who would listen.

So their time from learning these words from these beautiful souls within the forests was of the heaviest of hearts. This was not to be. This was an undoing of all that is sacredness itself. Skies grew angry with sadness and pain. Seas beat out their silent depths to speak with all life within it. Mountains called out unto the sun to ask for its warmth and light to shine more than it had ever before. The Orblings knew that this earth that creates and nurtures everything must now be nurtured before it was far too late.

***

When rested from their discoveries through the forests of earth, The Orblings arrived at the edge of a beautiful mountain range: some snow capped, some formed from rocks of many shapes and colours. There was a majesty, a place of consciousness that was inexplicable; nothing hidden upon the faces of its magnificences. All was to hold high for the face of humankind to look upon in all its wonder.

Life there called out to them. As they drew closer to rock, it began to explain about their world there and how they had suffered. 'The sun that gave the fertile earth life and wondrous plants is beginning to burn the air. All that is has become dry without water. Many here have perished from the heat that used to bring us warmth and nourishment but now is too much to bear without our rains to give us drink. Our skies have changed. That which nurtured us across all seasons is now becoming our enemy. We have watched so long how the greed and selfishness of humans is changing all that is. From the trees and sands and rock that form within our earth's mantle there is much pain for our Mother Earth.

'Our sacred mountains once held the beauty and oneness of life itself so that we could reach up to the skies to speak great things together. For such a long time we have struggled to survive. Some of us have lost the will to survive amid these times. Some of us have nothing left to sustain us. Others stay and persevere in the hope of good life again. But here we ask that you help us, please!

'Our strengths are powerful as we work as one throughout our planet. If all there is will be destroyed and abandoned, we will have lost more than it is possible to understand. Within us all are the substances of life past, present, future. To understand this is to see far beyond the universes, far beyond our fears and ignorances, far beyond our point of light, within that place that is infinite.'

While The Orblings blinked in amazement, they knew these words held all and everything that would never be undone. Just sitting in such a magnificence was to be with sacredness itself. As time passed across the closing light, The Orblings looked at each other with a quizzical smile. They knew this was one of their journeys that had to take them. All around listened to their words of wisdom that would hold them in great contentment. As they spoke with their gentle hands, a rainbow spread above them all. In silence everything moved in harmony to its place of being. There were no fears left upon their eyes, and light began its sleep. They knew then what they had to do, so it was.

***

Soon after arrival upon the shores of a far-off land that rested at the edge of a great sea, thoughts glided like nomadic birds above the day's coolness of its dawn. Here in soft silence, The Orblings sat on the beautiful, caramel sands of a beach lost along a transparent sea. Within moments a wall of froth and foam rolled in from the centre of the bay's swaying current. To their surprise, there came a dolphin. Dolphins being such shy creatures, this was incredible to behold. For The Orblings, though, things such as these would always be just how it should be for them. Dolphin swam up into the edge of the shoreline as if these two had always been in her life.

Upon speaking with The Orblings, Dolphin explained how her world of fabulous wonders beneath these waves was in the most fearful dangers from humanity. She told of days and nights that would bring about the destruction of her gentle world. How, over long years, that which lives and thrives within their forests in the seas is now so damaged that all that dwells there lives in a sadness that is more than they can bear.

'Every beautiful soul there is losing freedom and love within their heart. They hurt so badly now, that there is a silence that has descended upon their world. Everything is being torn away from their homes—homes that are being broken so that they can never again be loved places to live and grow. That which is left behind is devastation far too broken, so too our hearts. Families grown here for many lifetimes are gone now, or lost from each other's companionship, lonely and without anything they know. This world of waters is our sacredness,' Dolphin cried, 'because our realm is our place in this universe which is here to nurture this planet. We are humble and gentle souls. Our presence here is the combined forces upon this earth. We have always understood it is we who must teach how to live together.'

Be Strength

When you choose to learn how to be the best you can,
You can walk upon a path you know.
There will always be a guiding star
That shows you just who you really are.

It is all here upon this earth.
Look at all the beauty around.
It needs no money;
It has no greed.

Walk as a child upon this earth;
You will be as innocence.
Walk as a child upon this earth;
You will see beyond all time and space.

Long journeys take you places far from home;
There is this place in your heart that you can never roam.
When that stormy sky finds you,
Stand strong with everything you are.

Choose to be the best you can be;
It is all here upon this earth.
Look at all its beauty around.
It needs no money;
It has no greed.
It is peace.

With breath and being, you have much more than you can
dream.
Find your way in gentleness.
Find your way in love.
Find your way in humilities.
For you are all.

Come with me so we can grow together, little one;
You will teach me how.
Come with me so we will grow together, little one;
So we shall find all beautiful things in our loved and lovely
garden.

Come with me where every being grows together, little one;
You will teach me how.
Come with me so we choose to learn together, little one;
There we shall see all beautiful things in our loved and lovely
garden.

Come with me to help life laugh and dance together, little
one;
You will teach me how.
Let us go where we can shine so bright, little one;
Then we shall work so hard with all beautiful things in our
loved and lovely gardens.

Come with me with gentle hearts that love together, little
   one;
You will teach me how.
Come with me so sacredness itself creates all that is to be,
   little one;
While we shall live in harmony with all beautiful things in
   our loved and lovely gardens.

Come with me as one who has evolved together, little one;
You will teach me how.
Come with me, you of heart and soul together, little one;
Now we shall forevermore journey with all our beautiful
   things in our loved and lovely gardens.

Destination

I see a place that calls to me,
When life I cannot understand.
I feel my soul reach out,
When I am lost and wounded.
It finds my heart;
It soothes my tears;
It takes me home.

If you can find it in yourself today to be more than you were
    yesterday,
Then you have made your life good.
If you can help a little more today than you did yesterday,
Then you have made others' lives good.
If you can make the most from the little you had yesterday,
Then you have made your heart a better place.

If you can work harder today than you worked yesterday,
Then you have made light of a heavy load.
If you can hold out your hand when help is in need,
Then you have saved a good soul in this world.

If you can find it within yourself to understand that which is
    unknown,
Then you have learnt to become more than you believed.
If you can repay a friend for that deed they have done,
Then you have given that gift from your love.

If you can walk among fears today from your pain yesterday,
Then you have strength of warriors.
If you can inspire those who look down upon you,
Then you have become universe.

If you can protect that which is innocence as never before,
Then you have become that light that will allow all to see.
If you can forgive those who try to destroy with ignorance,
Then you can create all possibilities.

If you have given everything and more,
Then you learnt what life is meant to be.
If you have saved a soul from losing heart,
Then you have learnt how to truly see.

If you have walked in the shoes of poverty,
Then you will never again know fear.
If you have become someone you dreamt of being,
Then you have attained wisdom.

Where you journey with the eyes of a warrior,
Sacredness illuminates every step along your way.

The Wisdom of Time

Whatever the time,
It always lets us know.
When it's time for the flowers to grow,
It always seems to know.

'Tick tock,' says the clock.
Whenever it's time,
It always lets us know
When it's time for the grass to grow.

'Tick tock,' says the clock.
Whoever's in time,
It always lets us know
When it's time for little children to grow.

'Tick tock,' says your clock,
Waiting for us to know.
It always lets us know
When it's time for us to grow.

'Tick tock,' says our clock,
Wishing our lives away.
She always lets us know
When it's time we need to grow.

Listen to this clock.
Tick and tock,
Tick and tock.
When you hear its tick tock,
Listen with everything you are.
Look all around,
See what you have found.
Wait for the time;
She knows you will do just fine.
While things keep moving around,
Just see what you have found.
Wait for the ticking of time;
She always knows you will do just fine.

She keeps moving around;
Go see what you have found.
Listen with the ticking of time;
She sees you doing just fine.
Time for you to dream soon;
She is Mother Nature's clock.
Life will grow from her silvered moon.

Time to Grow Together

Night falls asleep upon my window.
She whispers, 'Time to sleep.'
Velvet dark of eyes and hair,
She holds my dreams within her keep.

We talk,
We dance,
We laugh about what we have learnt today.
We find ways to make tomorrow for helping friends.
We share my cocoa from our special cup,
Then fall into your world of dreams.

Goodnight, Miss Night!
I thank you so!
Please keep me safe and sound.
Goodnight, Miss Night!
I love you so!
Please keep me safe if I am lost.
Show those who love me where I can be found.

Your stars twinkle on my face;
I wear them like diamonds of light.
When you tap my window, all is well;
Then I know all is safe for me to dream tonight.

Night sleeps inside my room,
And all the world is breathing.
I wish her love.
I wish her the best that best can give.

Wherever those who need a friend,
I wish them help whenever needed.
Whoever's lost with no way home,
I call upon their angels.

With all I have,
With all I am,
I dream of our world.
To grow,
To learn,
To help,
To love.
We are here to grow;
We are here to learn;
We are here to help;
We are here to love.
We are all a piece of our place in this world.
We can only grow together.

Guardian

Life is a multitude of friends;
They know me well.
As we speak together in my dreams,
They teach me many things.

In our skies beautiful life flies to me;
They find me when I am far away.
As we speak together in my dreams,
They listen to what I wish to say.

In our skies beautiful life flies to me;
They find me when I am far away.
As we speak together in my dreams,
They bring me home to those I love.

In our skies beautiful life flies to me;
They find me when I am far away.
As we speak together in our dreams,
They know where I have travelled.

In our skies beautiful life flies to me;
They find me when I am far away.
As we speak together in my dreams,
They see my soul so well.

In our skies beautiful lives fly to me;
They find me when I am far away.
As we speak together in our dreams,
They hold my heart in gentleness.

In our skies beautiful beings walk with me;
They found me when I was far away.
As we always speak together in our dreams,
They will always be within my soul.

In our skies beauty will live with me;
It is my companion wherever I go.
As we dream within its dreams,
Home is there.
Home is this dream,
Loved by such beauty.
I am loved.
I am home.

In our skies beautiful angels fly with me;
They carry me when I am lost.
As we are one together in our dreams,
They watch over me.
When I need to rest,
They take me home.

In the seas worlds of beauty swim.
They are our guardians of the deep.
They are souls of countless dreams.

Sky of waters
Flow upon our fears.
Be the calmness of our minds;
Be the rivers of our tears.

All we are is lost,
Where this paradise discarded.
All we are is adrift,
Upon tides of eternities.

Sky of waters
Flow upon our fears.
Be the calmness of our minds;
Be the rivers of our tears.

Sky of waters
Flow upon our fears.
Be that calmness in our minds;
Be that river to carry our tears.

Sky of waters
Flow upon our fears.
Be this calmness for our minds;
Remember us in our hours of need.

Lights On

Rain on the windows.
Big old front door with its chips and cracked paint waiting;
Waiting for me to unlock and open up.
Silver metal shining from the peachy porch light;
And I am home.

Warm light sticks on my face.
Woollies hung in our lobby.
Boots, shoes, brollies clinging onto scarves.
Well-worn family friends,
They demand their own space

Looking back down the path,
Tiles glossy and glowing,
I close my front door.
Sleepy from discovering,
But smiling from knowing,
This is my home,
Where all give me love.
This is home.

Slipping off my weather-worn boots,
I smell coffee and toast.
It is where all that love abides,
In our kitchen of our togetherness,
Where we are dipped in contentment.
Cosy cakes and hot tea;
This is where every journey
Begins and ends for me.

Leathered couch in the corner;
If it could only speak.
Rest my head on its arm;
Let its cushions hold my feet.

Pastel colours glow from the cotton cloth on the table;
Glasses clink with soft, juicy drinks.
Our cats lounge in the armchairs;
Supper's scruffy dishes stacked in the sink.

Rugs flicker with hot shadows;
Logs crackle as if to laugh.
Butter arrives for our toast.
Our patient old clock ticks and tocks;
We all are here in our assortment of socks.
A home-made card sits on the busy mantle.
This is home where I can dream.

An Unusualness

Such a usual sort of day, or so I believed. My morning stroll over to my local park brought me back to my centred point in my cluttered mind. Just a few long strides down to the corner. Trees, huge skyscrapers, protecting the greenery and silent solitude of our community's little oasis of tranquillities.

A huge emerald-green, heavy ironed gate swung open in my cold hand. Rain speckled softly onto the red brick path. Squirrels watched nosily as they investigated corners of the woodland areas. Rooks and a cheeky assortment of birds were starting their breakfast menu. As I had decided on a short switch-off in silence moment, I headed briskly to my favourite bench overlooking the bowling green. Those breakfast-club birds kept one eye on me until I froze in situ, then casually went about their selections of juicy morsels, minding their own business.

'Here George!' shouted the taller of the two.

'With you!' replied the other.

Meeting back together, I could see that they had one of those litter pickers and had found an ideal snatch moment they both wanted to be a part of. This was a rare event I didn't quite believe.

'Hi there!' one of them shouted over, watching me watching her. It was one of those awkward times when you did not want to seem as if you are being a nosy parker.

'Hi! It is so good to see someone taking it upon themself to clean up their environment.'

'Oh yes! It's what we do! We know how important looking after our world is. Everyone can do something.'

'My goodness! That's so true! But I have never seen anyone do this *here* before, apart from the park warden.'

'Not surprised. There are so many good people on this earth who wish to do great things, but connecting them all is not as simple as it seems,' added the girl.

'We decided, how about we just make a start somewhere where we live, in some little way or other?' said the boy, who was by now sitting just opposite me on the bowling green.

'So where would you like to go from here?'

'Oh, sorry! My name is Ruby. Pleased to meet you.'

'Mine is Daisy! And this is Dennis!' replied the tall girl.

'A great duo!' I said.

We all laughed as if we had known each other forever.

'Dennis is my brother. He's the elder by one year, but as you can see, I was blessed with height.'

We laughed again as Daisy made herself comfortable next to her brother.

'Our dream is to develop a network of fabulous individuals who can be an integral part of a creative network, and through its own magic create a unique system of communications, and by this create the means to call upon individuals who possess different skills. These will then be compiled and catalogued, with the aim of growing a powerful database of like-minded people who will be there to call upon for their skills.'

I was in awe of these two incredible individuals, so full of giving for the sake of our planet that I was lost for words, temporarily that is. 'Is this something just the two of you are part of then, or are there more of you?' I asked excitedly.

Daisy replied with an eagerness in her voice that was rich with a strength and wisdom much more than her years. 'Well, it all started with an afternoon conversation over coffee and cake. We had been having ideas together for months previously about how we could actually create a practical way of connecting individuals with the purpose of growing a network of beautiful souls who wish to nurture all and everything in our world. Their skills and abilities will be our building blocks to utilise, along with their dreams of how we can create the best and most sustainable ways of living creatively.'

'That was exactly our dream!' Dennis added, with his funny little wisp of a curl that fell in his eye. 'Over these months we have held on to our dream, adding this and that until we chose to begin this conversation in our outdoor arenas. This park is on our doorstep. This is a great starting point to open the windows, as it were. Yesterday was our litter pick through our block of terraces. Already we have made seven acquaintances who are now litter picking two other parks in our area. They, along with their friends, have called the word out to other like-minded individuals who are today beginning a compilation of individuals who wish to be a part of our dream; thus, any skills, abilities, ideas or dreams will be logged and the foundations of our nurturement of earth is being seeded. For those who have specific abilities, we can brainstorm with all to utilise in specific ways. Those with all and every skill, we can blend across those needs to strengthen any lacks or imbalances in our communities.'

Daisy then nodded to Dennis with a comforting smile. 'You see? Togetherness is where we can build that which is not in place. Every being has skills, abilities and individualities that are completely unique to that individual. It is, and has been, as this all along, but humans do possess this wasting ability that can and does destroy that which nurtures us as a species. Some choose to become this destroyer in the full knowledge of what the consequences are. Others – us – choose to become at one with all that is nurturement. We have to learn by degrees. Within this learning we become more than we were. More than anything we could ever have imagined. There is no doubt we can be destroyers, and there become less than we are. What then happens is those who destroy and live as this become destroyed by their own deeds and creations. It is a sacredness which is all and protects as warriors protect that which is sacredness itself.' But then Dennis knew that all that his sister had said was everything that he too knew to be the way things were meant to be.

With the sound of each word spoken by the two, I realised this was the miracle I had been longing for. So long I had been wishing, dreaming, for a way to begin this creating communities, creating oneness, planting the healing seeds in order to allow growth, nurturement of healing. Is it humans as a race who are so lost within themselves that we cannot nurture that which nurtures the species? If we are to rise above this self-imposed prison, then it is the species itself that must become and overcome that which is the element of destruction. Understanding is more than mere cataloguing facts. Intelligence has many levels of substances that in themselves are compartmentalised. This accumulation of facts is mechanical, without senses, robotic and unemotional. Nurturement lives within the heart, mind, soul and spirit of beings. Beings with intelligence far beyond this realm live to achieve that sacredness unknown to those who are prisoners of their unconsciousness. Everything that permeates through this filter of unconsciousness is only superficialness tormented by its own ego.

Time passed in the park so quickly as I listened to the two talk about their incredible dreams of a nurturing world, possibilities of creating wonderful ways of living only dreamt of; but this dream is the possibility that would prove to be magical. This requires our abilities to align billions of grains of individualities into a living, breathing, moving, feeling entity. To connect with, to communicate with, to cooperate with, to converse with, to coexist within one beautiful entity called humanity. With individuality there is uniqueness. Uniqueness creates special abilities. What one individual has within themselves, another has a different design specific to them. Time is given to us as a journey to be continued. One day cannot be as the last. If it is, there cannot be change. We live in the Orb of change, to create possibilities within. Here, this day, we are creating possibilities. What they are, depend on us. Our intelligence can determine what and how we wish to achieve.

So it was, that walk in my park had to be. It held everything in its bigger picture. Daisy and Dennis kept in touch with me about anything and everything we made happen. We learnt never to take anything for granted. It was up to us to see life's potentials. After all, we had no other options.

Networks were designed for the specific individualities of any given ability, skill or natural creativity. We decided on colour-coding these categories for compatibility, to how easily they would be able to work together at any given time. Those individuals who were time rich, we gave priority to for creating the foundations of the nurturement Orbs. For those who were time poor, but were highly skilled at their trades, we designed our networking hub, to recognise priorities in our 'seedlings'; these then would magnetise themselves on to any particular root system. The Mother Root is our origin Orb which guides and nurtures all incomers to their feeding root. Individuals with incomprehensible abilities, once identified, would have the new seed connect with them, logging and communicating that new information along the root to awaiting established seeds. Our stem is the artery where the life blood flows, carrying individual seeds that have that endless potential to create and instigate creation.

Now established, we are building the canopies of the Tree. This will be Tree, the accumulated intelligences of countless individualities connecting, communicating, creating, consciously nurturing each grain of all that is within themselves, as well as within all that can be. Within Tree are our endless potentials of each grain of us as a species. One grain can inspire another. One thought can merge into another's. One passion can construct that vehicle to transport another's hopes, wishes and dreams across any obstinate obstacle that has grown deep within another's psychological maelstrom of human maladies.

***

Black, white, differences of similarities. History is just that. History is humanity's living entity of past and present and is the sole receiver of humanity's physical, emotional and spiritual sculpturing of the clay of time for a particular species—this species. This diversity of such a specific species is, as most, exceptional. Individualities are a uniqueness, as every species. We apparently are the most advanced since discovering the means to survive, adapt and live throughout a passage of time: time that we now understand as being our mirror to those actions that some of us are at a loss to understand. A need to survive is all-encompassing, but what we are is a species that has been given the uniqueness of specific abilities: abilities that can create and build from numerous sources on our planet. We then are able to communicate throughout many species for the greater good. This communication carries the seeds of either negativity or positivity that will affect endless strata of existence. It is our gift of choice that will decide how we wish to impact our lives and the internal architecture of our lives we design. What we dream, we have the capabilities to replicate into our consciousness. Intent is our compass that will guide our conscience. Whether it be for evil, legacy shall charter your course to sacredness; whether it be for good, the gravity of your conscience shall allow you to reach the heavens. What we are then are guardians of this world's dream of returning home.

Our Purpose

Do not look for me,
Because I am not here.
The whys and the wherefores are of no concern.
It is a calling of my soul
That finds me wanting for the freedom.

I am the navigator of all existence within.
It is a mighty warrior of highest heavens.
All that is will unveil unto its nth degree.
And so it is, I am its willing vessel.

Will you live within your deepest honours,
Where that place doth call upon your soul?
For I will be there, my dearest friend.
Then we can work together;
Live all those things that our dreams have always told.

Now look upon the brightest star that shines for you tonight;
It is your mind's salvation.
All so bright has all and more to restore your soul;
It will belong to us to light with our communications.

So long awaiting, though still it shines for you;
While here this world is lost amid wounded dreams
That only we can allow to fly free once more.
But so we can with every waking moment.
It is within our reach,
As is within our dreams.

Will you listen here from your highest mountain?
I call upon you, be strong,
Be well,
Be all and more your being,
For we are here to guide this realm.

Rewrite Our Past

Write your pages in your history books
While your passing of time calls your names,
Remember to describe all those wonderful things
That you could never speak of without shames.

Let now your story be told upon many a good soul's wisdom.
To let this here be undone
Is to fall and never to learn to rise.
For our beautiful and sacred world,
She waits for us to see.
She waits for us to let her be magnificence.

Where are all our sacred stars that gave this life?
They dwell within us to set us free;
They are waiting for your eyes to see.
With lights so beautiful,
They hold your light so patiently.
Time to give with all those colours you are;
Time to give love and be that star.
Your journey has sown a universe of stars.

Write beneath your light the pages of your history.
You will need to see
With every word you live.
With every word, be aware.

History is written from the dreams we have invited.
Those pages are sometimes too heavy to turn.
Dare we look into the shadowed places of our minds,
So there to hold the light?
Be not afraid of dreams within our nights.
Be there to hold the light.

Warrior of Peace

Be at peace here,
In the quiet of your mind,
For all you are is here.
Within this earth there holds a shard of sacred light.

You have found far more than which was lost;
Walk silent within your solitude.
Here then will you be at peace with fears.
Be at peace here,
In the quiet of your mind.

Your journey has come full circle;
Where you once knew has returned.
Each step will teach you which way you need to go;
Your sacredness will teach you all that you need to know.

There is a force beyond this place of heart,
Where all is known.
Be with your strength, as this will guide you home.
Can you be that which these magical stars illuminate?

It is of you I call upon to give more than lifetimes.
Walk here with understandings,
With humilities,
With love,
With being.

It is that which was;
It is that which is;
It is that which shall be;
It is that which must return.

There is a time when we cannot remain,
Into a place where the fabrics of mind and space collide.
Strength will be our shield.
Wisdom will be our sanctuary.

It is such a short journey into our ignorances.
We can walk or we can run.
If we choose, we can just be still;
And there become a warrior.

With sky I move upon the searching breeze;
In breath and body I hold this light.
Listen here as it awaits your fleeting memories
Of what you are.

To find our way into another dawn,
Lift your eyes unto each new horizon.
Feel the silence of eternities.
Be there amid all sufferings, to protect with all you are.

As innocence walks into your journeys to be that strength
When those who cannot find their ways upon their fearful
    paths,
Find your place across each desolation.
Be there when no one else will hold that light.

While this world moves with our heartbeat,
We must shine upon those who need find their way home.
In our sharing our journey upon this realm of imaginations,
Our world will be returned to this point,
Our givers of light.

Wait upon the emptiness of those who will not give.
Create that which has been left with nothing.
Nurture all with the coming of your sight;
Life will flow there,
As the coming of day upon the darkest night.

Was it you I met throughout another life?
I saw you then;
I found you now.
This world stood still,
Like silence past a storm;
So I will be here to hold that light.
I shall always find our way back home.

But all that was has left behind,
As if an echo from my mind's eye.
There I found all but love,
Though I found my solace.

Somewhere some solace held my hand,
And I did cry so bitterly.
To feel at peace with hard-found company,
I was so free.

When all had gone,
Torn into my heart once more,
To know some peace, such hard-found company,
I lived to feel so free.

No need to fear that where you are now;
I know your heart.
As I have lived so many lives,
There are all more to be.
Come now, for we have much to learn.

Together

Where this is all we have to give,
For this is everything of how we are meant to live.
Step quiet now, for we can move between the breeze,
Here, while we cried for loss and sanities.

We call that light to shine upon our way;
We call the beating heart.
We call our souls to show us all the way.
We then can find our paths of nurturement;
We then return ourselves to find where we start.

I carry the light,
So here I stay.
Before my mind is lost,
I carry this light to find my way.

I dare hold this light
With heart and soul,
With all my mortal might.
Let worlds grow forevermore;
Yet more than more,
I only fear abandonment of courage.

Here shall be the place where life will find its chance;
And so I watch with angels upon the skies,
To fly among our stars,
And all the while allow their beauty.

Flow like a river upon our world;
Be that miracle.
Shine like a thousand stars within our sky,
Where everything we live gives love.

Find me. I am the sky.
Where you look up I am there.
Lose your way among fearful times.
There is nothing more that can harm you;
Nothing but your love remains there.

Be all with your heart;
Open each door that holds you within.
Create the key;
Set yourself free.

Sifting through those corners,
Take all the time you need.
You are here now.
Your journey must pause.

Dreams will show you how to live,
In breath,
In beat of heart,
In blink of eye,
In sound,
In feelings,
In movement of our intents,
In choice,
In mind,

In thought,
In intent,
In strength,
In weakness,
In overcoming,
In strength,
In believing,
In understanding,
In being that strength,
In understanding beyond this illusion,
In being.

See with your soul;
Universe is awaiting.
Our stars cascade from mind,
To shine with all they are.

Illuminate those fears with strength;
Rise above your sufferings.
Where all that leave their emptiness,
Learn to feel that silent sacredness.
It is here within.
Lift your eyes towards that silence,
And all there is shall be all that is.

So fall when all you are is lost;
Your soul shall shine its light.
So fall when all you are is lonely;
Your soul shall forever be your light.

Nothing here will be abandoned;
We carry you safe within eternities.
When life leaves you lost and torn,
We carry you home.

Here on this moment of this, our path,
We listen to understand
Whether to work together in unity,
Or become inspiration through all you are,
Or to cling to the burdens of ignorances.
Be your dreams.

We Are One

Step into the night while you look for your understanding.
There, in this distance of your heartaches,
As a lighthouse upon the shore,
It will guide you home again.

Here in this moment
We can share this gift.
In working together in our nature and unity,
With each new day given,
We must learn.
In that learning,
We must grow.
At the end of a day,
We must find our way.
Such a long walk to freedom.
We must be that much betterment
Tomorrow.

When all you have is loss,
Share its burdens;
For in that sharing you become more.
Then give your wisdoms to those in need,
And you will no more hunger.

As one,
We are strength.
In working together,
We are hope.
In speaking together,
We are knowledge.
In listening together,
We are understanding.
In giving together,
We are more.
In walking together,
We are love.
In creating together,
We are the seeing.
We are being.
In communicating togetherness,
We are one.

Child

You have everything you ever need;
Time here to be the nurturement you are.
It is forever with you;
Believe it is never far.

When you play in the park,
See all that surrounds you.
Be that energy passed on to me,
So now I give to you.

Breathe this air which nurtures you;
Open all the windows of your mind.
Allow beautiful colours to flow into your eyes.
When you need to find your answers,
You will indeed be pleased.

Walk into your day.
Take with you all your being.
Create from the depths of your soul.
Give with integrity;
Give with humilities;
Give with love.

Child of this earth,
Shine with your light of innocence.
Shine so bright that the stars will smile forever.
Child of this earth, share your light,
Share this pureness,
Share this love,
Until you become all that you are meant to be.

Be silent when you are feeling sad;
Listen to its heartbeat around you.
Be still when you are feeling frightened;
You will be protected by those who care.

Child of this world's gentleness,
Make your words kind.
Hold each moment of your day into the light,
Then see how your love makes everything around you bright.

It is what you dream.
It is how you nurture them.
It is that devotion.
It is the bridge to your heavens.

Child of this world,
Become the stars that will light this world.
Just learn those things that you will understand.
There you shall be the magic
Our world is waiting for.

Who are we anyway?
Do we ever really know?
Are we here?
Are we there?
Is what we see really there?
Or are we seeing what we wish to see?
Because we dare not unmask,
Just in case we don't like what's there.

Could it be we are something that we have lost?
Is there a description on a tag?
Something strange in a box?
Might we be a distant memory?
Or something familiar we remember in a dream?

Should we research our history?
Would we like what we would see?
Can there be someone who might know
Just who do you think it could be?
Was there an important reason?
Will you ask someone who might know?

Is this our journey into the unknown?
Will it be a scary place?
And who will look back from that mirror there?
I wish it to be my face.

Where can we make some improvements?
I don't have many skills,
But what I can I do quite well.
If there is something fabulous to create,
I know that I would not hesitate,
And do good I will.

Life may fit you like a glove,
Or a worn-out hat,
A torn-up glove.
But for now make your peace with what you are.
This is your face in these veiled reflections.
I see your heart;
I feel your soul.
I will nurture your spirit.

STARFISH

Moonlight sifted silver stars down through the warmth
And turquoise of the crystal sea.
Starfish resting softly,
Smiling as she slept
On her coral ledge.
So beautiful,
So happy to be that starfish,
Where all her friends lived together around her.
All the work was made as a game.

***

From day to day everything had a feeling that each being
felt. But they did not have to say anything about this feeling;
they just knew it existed each and every day they worked
hard together. Working was never any hardship for them.

The more they worked to look after each other and their
environment, the more they wished to work for the good of
all. Within those working hours, which were usually from
around and after sun up until just a jot before lunching time,
it was a thing that work was to be fun, as well as functional.
So what would wrap itself around any rather laborious odds
and ends was a warm wave of happiness. It was that
wondrous feeling that held on to any feeling of being alone.
Happiness filled the smallest of beings to the largest of
mighty beings. Indescribable it was; no matter what, working
together in any capacity changed the heaviest of chores into
the lightest of things to create better things. Simple as that.
What had been achieved in this wondrous community was
nothing short of miraculous. To this community it was, and

is, what humans would call normal, though for us reading this, we know that to live such as this is a very wonderful way for any being – such a very wonderful way indeed. Stories told here, in this beautiful, magnificent and wonderful community, are magical stories filled with something indescribable. It is hard work in any place to discover that being industrious each day can be incredibly happy.

With each day passing, working as one great team is building something special within and without the fabric of this undersea universe; nothing short of magical. With each moment passing, they have discovered what working together really means.

Here, with the working, sharing, nurturing, caring, knowing of what each being is giving into their lives, is where and how the sacred seeds of nurturement are born into that which is eternal and most beautiful. Colours of every kind shimmer within this world of sharing and caring, growing most fabulous with the beat of every good heart. Of all sizes and of all that move in different ways. Of all that speak with different sounds. Of all that look in differences, that are like jewels that reflect sacredness itself. We are the same.

In Our Hands

For good or bad,
Where only you can say.
And in the moment, we have that chance,
Such a chance to be part of magic for a day,
All will give to those who give their all,
With dreams s to soothe our hardships.
And if we wish to see inside our faltered stars,
If you have learnt much more than life reveals,
Then love will lift all burdens from your eyes.

Give with the beating of your heart;
Be its force of love.
Wish this with each beat that keeps you here upon this earth,
Then wake from every thought.

With passing words our memories hold our dreams.
There, without greatness, we have nothing we can define.
A fallen world has need of everything with love.
It is such sacredness of this,
That every deed will carve its mark upon the face of time.

Where all those forces be,
I wait upon that frightful soil.
Where all those forces be,
I am that which has no fears.
I walk amid my dreams.

For you see
I am the earth of immortalities.
None shall hide from the coming of this light.
I am the skies of dreams that bear impossibilities.
Nothing that was,
Nothing that is,
Nothing that shall be can shield.

Here time has found itself
To ask your soul to choose its path.
Walk within your purpose to find your heart
There, and future will endure.
So believe in all the goodness you do;
Today is where this way of being can start.

And in that waiting, there is a peace:
The knowing of some other-worldly something
Hidden inside another parallel,
A parallel of us.
Our need is such that we must
Align with sacredness.

In all fates we arrive at the same point in this universe:
Fantastical consciousness and consequence.
Too soon this light shall cease to sift upon our incandescence.
Within one soul lies the stars to birth this universe,

And yet we will not look into our hearts
To learn how we can nurture all
To live within its light.
And all shall know when all converges.

I watch from times unageing,
To gather safe such immortalities
That they may breathe their life,
To resurrect our history
Then understand how to live in the present.

Be As Innocence

Walk as a child;
Look upon the smallest being
With wonderment.
Walk as a child;
In this world
Throughout those next.

While many times you falter,
Our learning comes with wisdoms.
Walk as a child;
Then you can find this place.
Where life is just another destination,
The skies will know your name.

In your quiet knowing,
Listen to your soul.
It shall hold all this universe
Inside your mind.
It will speak with silence
When you let free your heart.

Walk as a child;
Look upon the smallest being with knowing.
Walk as a child;
This earth will know you.

Lift your soul to meet the skies,
With thought,
With senses,
With the beating of your loving heart.

And there am I.
There I shall meet you always,
So far journeyed but always to return.
By many thoughts
I travel where I wish to be.

Walk as a child;
Look upon each being with love,
With understanding,
With compassion.
You will be shown the same.
Walk as a child;
This universe has forever known your name.

It Is Nearly Tomorrow

We are the ones who hold the light;
There is this calling of the Orb.
Where all that is requires healing;
It is a dawning of us warriors of souls.

Reach into that which grows each grain of love.
Search deeply as to feel your journeys of fears.
There is nothing that can harm you there,
If you believe impossibilities become reality.

For here is your heart;
For here is your soul;
For here you are stars of our skies;
For here you are every reason why.

In your sight shines the path to your destinations;
In your mind lives the place of your salvations.
In your heart beats the sounds of your convictions;
In your soul dwells the gates of your redemptions.

For in that silence,
We have the sight.
You will find your way
Far beyond this realm.
Where senses of this earth are lost,
There we will hold that star:
Our star that we thought was lost
But no one cared enough,
And so it hid away and fell.

It is watching all your journeys:
Where we choose to follow,
Who we believe we are,
How we live our lives.
It shines upon us when we fall asleep.

When you have become one with all that is,
There illuminates your past and present.
You have the universe within your mind.
This answer dwells within your eyes.

This Place of Empathy

I see a strength within your eyes.
What then could you have seen?
I hear that strength within your voice;
Life has given you more than wealth.
There is sound upon your words;
They for those who are forgotten.

Are you the colours in my mind
That take me to a special place?
Are you that sound in my quiet
That fill me with humilities?

Were you the memories that held my heart
In those fearful places I used to hide?
Were you that feeling I could not describe
But all along I knew you were always there?

Did I cross your mind sometimes,
To fill your eyes with tears?
Did I change your life for the betterment?
If in doing so,
Have I helped you see?

Where does all this love vanish to?
But does it not leave some lasting trace,
Where love is given with all its grace?
I know.
It is here,
In my heart.
It waits within tomorrow.

Ask me how to give;
I will show you how to care.
Ask me how to live;
I will show you how to see.
Ask me how to understand;
I will unlock your heartaches.
So that you can then be free.

I see strength within your eyes;
I understand what you have seen.
Your strength has risen from the ashes;
And here you can choose just when to fly.

The Place of Alignments

Open your eyes, little child;
There is a new day waiting.
Open your eyes, little child;
Here you are,
Come to give all the beauty you can give.

Open your eyes, little child;
This is the best day awaiting.
Open your eyes, little child;
Here you are,
Come to see all the beauty you can give.

Open your eyes, little child;
Here is the sunshine for your smile.
Open your eyes, little child;
Here you are, growing just fine,
Coming to grow all the seeds you plant each day.

Open your eyes, little child;
Be that new page in your story.
Open your eyes, little child;
Here you are,
Coming to create another book for us to read.

Open your eyes, little child;
Live with all the love that you can hold.
Open your eyes, little child;
You are here with me,
Ready to make this new day the best you have ever known.

Open your eyes, little child;
Be awake to build your brightest stars.
Open your eyes, little child;
Everything in this world is waiting.

Open your eyes, little child;
Come with me, and I will help you grow.
Open your eyes, little child;
How special you are.
You can teach me how to be that child,
So we will learn together.

Open your eyes, little child;
Teach me how to become you.
Open your eyes, little child;
Please can I come with you,
To always keep our spirits safe in togetherness?

Come walk with me today;
You know wonderful places to see.
Come walk with me today;
I will laugh with you, and you with me.

Come walk with me today;
You have so much good to give.
Come walk with me today;
I can learn a new way to live.

Come walk with me today;
You are my shining light.
Come walk with me today;
I need your unceasing purity of sight.

Come walk with me today;
You will show me how to live.
Come walk with me today;
I wish to know what gifts I too can give.

Come walk with me today;
You found what I always dreamt.
Come walk with me today;
You are my angel heaven has sent.

Come walk with me today;
You are the sunshine through a stormy day.
Come walk with me today;
With you I return home, and here I stay.

Come walk with me today;
You are my heart and soul.
Come walk with me today;
You fill my world with light

Come walk with walk with me today
You fill each star with magic as I fall into night.

Come walk with me today;
You show me what life can be.

Come walk with me today;
I will walk with you,
So I can understand how to see.

Come walk with me today,
Angel that has entered our lives.
Come walk with me today;
You are the reason our earth will thrive.

You are forever that which shows us how to live.
It is you who the skies shine for.
It is you we can learn all there is and more.

That day when you took your first breath,
I had been waiting for you for so long.
When I saw you
I know that you saw me.
Only then did I understand.

To love without beginnings,
To love eternally,
To love with all you are,
Is to heal that which needs to mend.
That day when you joined my life,
I learnt just what love is for.

To love without beginnings,
To love with wisdoms,
With strengths,
To love with all you are,
Is to share that next beat of your heart.

That day when you held my hand,
I discovered the universe in my hand.
To love without beginnings,
To love eternally,
To love with all you are,
Is to heal that which is to be.

That day when you called my name,
I understood what life is for.
To love from the depth of your soul,
To love with passion and pain of loss,
Is to heal all the wounds that will make whole.

That day when you talked with me,
I cried from your innocence.
To love with no beginnings,
To love with only eternities,
To love with your very being.

Stars in the darkest night skies,
You will shine as they.
With all you are, our children,
We can now find our way.
Long paths lead to places we cannot see.
So much can happen,
So much unforeseen.
In many times we lose our ways,
Though we can find our light
If we choose.
That will return us to our soul's home,
This sanctuary of home.

Tomorrow Awaits

This life is but a journey,
Fragile as the frailest glass,
So little to make it shatter.
With the ebbing of time,
It cannot be undone.
Once broken, there is your chance to mend.
If you wish to live within your spirit,
There have found that special friend.

While all that see beyond their fleeting minds,
There are angels watching through fearful times.
With love as their shield of warriors,
They shall be with you.
As this earth transcends,
Our chance to change our hearts will be waiting.

It is the now.
It is the time.
It is all-knowing.
It is that which is.

As a river it nurtures your being;
Be the strength that binds your love.
As a mountain carries your soul;
Be the voice that whispers above
the clouds.
Though in this moment of your living,
Life calls for your higher self,
It has not been,
Nor ever will,
To walk within the halls of humilities;
There to look upon this sacredness of life.
As this is yours,
And yours alone, to choose.

Hold out your hand, my child;
I am here to take you home.
Nothing to fear any more;
You shall never be alone.

Hold out your hand, my child;
I live inside your heart.
Night has returned to hold you safe;

Angel Child

Tomorrow is waiting for you to return;
There we will make a brand-new start.
Hold out your hand, my child;
While I wrap you warm in your cosy bed.
Tomorrow will always know
Just where you are to be found.

Hold out your hand, my child;
I will read a story to call your magical world,
And all your adventures of this lovely day.
Throughout the night
It will work to make all that love grow.
Your eyes will be filled with beautiful seeds,
To journey into your new day,
With everything wonderful to plant again.

Hold out your hand, my child;
I have returned to take you home.
Nothing more to fear any more;
You shall never be alone.

For all your stars are waiting,
To sprinkle you with love.
Here all your stars are waiting,
Shining down from your heavens above.

Hold out your hand, my child;
I will keep you safe for beyond time.
Hold out your hand, my child;
You are my angel.
When I am lost,
You hold my hand,
And there my fears are all just fine.

How to Love

To live with purpose;
To live with humility;
To live with a sense of our incredibilities;
To live with compassion for all that is.

To learn how to create;
To nurture all this greatness;
To protect innocence and love.

To give where there is poverty;
To be there when you find loneliness;
To choose integrities if there is greed;
To teach wisdom where there is ignorance;
To live and give without taking;
To create a uniqueness of your mind;
To allow life's beauty to grow.

So in this world we can understand why we are here.
It is for us to nurture this planet,
To be more than we believe we are.
We have the chance to live as one humanity,
To return this earth to its paradise.
There is a time that has arrived.
It cannot wait for unconscious minds.

We have a chance to wake from our dreams,
Those dreams that wait for us.
It is now we need to carry them into this world
With care, for they are sacred.

To planting wisdom
In abundance,
Creating its security,
Nurturing its heart and soul,
Protecting its existence,
Understanding where we need to go from here,
Learning why we are here,
Communicating as one being,
Looking for that new horizon
Where the sun awaits.

Everything We Are

Home is this place where my heart belongs,
Safe and secure,
With a big snuggly couch
Where we all sit and chat
About this,
About that.
The big old fireplace warms the cold nights
While we sit and we chat
About this,
About that,
While its red glow flickers
On our polka-dot macs
And we tell our day's stories
Through the hot chocolate haze.
That packet of biscuits
Is scoffed in a flash;
But we never need worry,
There's always a stash.
Soon the smell of fresh curry
Wafts from the kitchen door.
We all look at each other
Knowing we'll be asking for more.
Fridays are always our favourite nights;
Our living room looks like a fairy grotto,
Because we've decked it in lights.
Where we laugh and we cry
While our cats saunter by
Here and there.

After our home-made meal
There's a movie that steals
All our senses of logic,
Though we wouldn't miss it
For all the money in the world,
Because home is where everything
We are belongs.

And the whole world passes through
The affairs of the world:
Why people do what they do,
Fantastical events,
Both the good and the bad.
We laugh, and we cry,
Hug our friends
As we say goodbye
And come back soon.
When evening starts to shine silver,
We say, 'Here comes our moon!'

Kitchen sink stacked,
They can wait until morning,
When the kettle has boiled
And we have all stopped yawning.
One of us will always say,
'Cuppa time?
How many for a brew?'
While all the time
Every one of us knew,
We wouldn't miss this
For all the money in this world,
Because home is where everything
We are belongs.

And our whole world wraps around us,
Quiet and gentleness,
Without a sound.
Slippers all toasty,
Smiles on our cups,
Frosty glitter sprinkled
On our window sills.
Radio singing
To send us to bed,
And we all snuggle a big cuddle,
So as to send beautiful dreams
That we need in our world,
As we all know we do.
Then we wouldn't forget these
For all the money in our world.

Whoever is up first
Will always pave the way
By making great toast,
'Extra thick,' we all say,
And brewing our favourite coffee
In the most scrumptious way.
Clothes fresh and ready,
Soap suds in our hair,
Dancing around the living room rugs,
'Cause we just don't have a care.
And we are there,
Together forever,
No airs or graces;
They wouldn't fit on our sleepy faces.
We look after each other;
All this love grows our hearts,
Like big balloons
Floating in a summer's sky.

And we really do know why:
Because home is the very best place to be.
So we wouldn't change this
For anything but love.
It is all we ever need
In this whole wide world.

Our place called home,
Where we wouldn't wish
To be anywhere else.
But then we knew we wouldn't,
Not for all the wealth
In the wealth of this world,
Because home is where
We have much more
Than wealth allows.
Home is where everything
We are belongs.

ords Unmask

Write your story words
So that we can read
And learn what you have said.

Write your story words
So that we can read
And understand much more.

Write your story words
So that we can read
And learn what is needed.

Write your story words
So that we can read,
And in that reading
See.

Write your story words
So that we can read,
And in that reading
Hear.

Write your story words
So that we can read,
And in that reading
Feel.

Write your story words
So that we can read,
And in that reading
Understand.

Write your story words
So that we can read,
And in that reading
Learn.

Write your story words
So that we can read,
And in that reading
Know.

Write your story words
So that we must read,
And in this reading
Heal.

Write your story words
So that we will read,
And in our reading
Create.

hen

When we come together
And see what we have always had,
Then we shall be alive.

When we look into each other's eyes
And feel that which we have always had,
Then we shall be alive.

When we work together
And realise what we have always had,
Then we shall be alive.

When we give to each other's hearts
And understand that which we have always had,
Then we shall be alive.

When we listen together
And realise what we have always had,
Then we shall be alive.

When we learn together
And understand that which we have always had,
Then we shall be alive.

When we create together
And heal everything more than we ever have,
Then we can live.

In this living
We can breathe from
Life that will grow
Diversities of our planet.
Infinite and inspirational,
Her sacred mantle will restore.
Taking shall be replaced.

By our giving;
By our living.

In consciousness,
Destruction rebuilt
By our willingness
To solve this imbalance
Which we have always allowed.
Now we understand
Our task is to restore balance,
We can help,
Through all possibilities,
To evolve.

Emerald Sky

Above my mind
I feel your heart calling to me.
Above my mind
You walk amid a faraway land.

Above my mind
I hear your soul calling to me.
Above my mind
You search amid a faraway land.

Above my mind
I see your eyes cry for me.
Above my mind
You drift amid a faraway land.

Above your mind
I feel my heart calling to you.
Above your mind
I walk amid a faraway land.

Above your mind
I hear my mind calling to you.
Above your mind
I search amid a faraway land.

Above your mind
I see my eyes cry for me.
Above my mind
I search amid a faraway land.

As we are lost,
Make it be upon the same path;
Then we shall follow
Within our knowing.

We shall get there,
That place where
All our dreams await.
They are the keepers of the gates,

Where all our longings
Find their sacred fates.
There, as our stars above
Sleep contented in the skies,
Here is where we find ourselves.

I Wish

If there is a place where we can speak,
But speak with a voice that knows just what to say,
I wish to be there.

If there is a past that we can learn from
And understand our mistakes along the way,
I wish to be there.

If there is a future waiting with our healing,
Every moment creating beauty for all that is,
I wish to live it.

If there is a day where we understand our being,
May it last forever throughout time.
I wish to see it.

I wish to speak from heart and soul;
I wish to learn to live.
I wish to heal this world with love;
For this is all I have to give.

I wish to grow like a mighty oak tree
And feed the soil,
So life can grow
With all that love to feed it.

Then we can be a forest
That in turn
Will feed everything around;
And in that giving,
Others then know that they can give,
So their children will grow strong
And they too will reach for the skies
With wisdom,
With humility.

And all this world will look upon your eyes
If you just be the best you can.
Grow with those who love you,
Then you will hold the seeds of forests
Within your hands.

Reach toward the skies, my children;
Wish with everything you are.
Allow yourselves to be the best you can be.
Be infinite;
Be that sacred star.

Mirror of Life

This earth is our reflection;
She is our mirror to our lives.
We have the key
To unlock the door of fates.

With how we nurture,
With how we care,
With how we consciously
Sense how we need to share.

This earth is our reflection;
She is the mirror to our lives.
We have this sight,
And with it
We must learn to see.

This earth is our reflection;
She lives for us
So that we can live.
We have the wisdom
Through dreadful legacies
And now have learnt
How to unchain
This innocence
That must be freed.

This earth is our reflection;
She is the mirror of our lives.
We have the key
To now unlock
The doors of fate.

It's time to nurture,
It's time to share,
It's time to wake;
Evolve ourselves
From perpetuating
Our own nightmares.

This earth is our reflection;
She shows us
How to live our lives.
We have always held the key,
But now we must
Set free our selfishness
To allow our skies
To find us with its love.
She is strong;
But that mirror of her soul
Is as fragile as our veil of immortalities.

Earth Bridge

Always ask what you can do,
No matter how small;
And in the asking
You will see
How to help us all.

Our earth,
Our skies,
Our seas.
Our understanding
Just what it takes
To take care of everything.

Always ask what you can do,
No matter where you are.
And in this asking
You will be
The magnificent shining star.

Upon our earth,
Within our skies,
Beneath our seas,
You find understanding
Of just what it takes
To take care of everything.

Always ask what you can do,
And in this asking
You will know
Just how to help us all.

Upon our earth,
Throughout our skies,
Beneath our seas,
You are given understanding
Of all it takes
To love and nurture everything.

Always ask, 'Can I become?'
Nothing is too insignificant.
For in your asking,
You will bring about
Our new world of
Earth's evolvement.

Your voice will be our compass,
Your words our chosen path.
Your being earth's strength and wisdom,
Your deeds her universal heart.

Dearest Friend,

Join me in this journey.
I need that someone to hold my hand.
Join me in life's journey.
If you wish
We can travel to faraway lands,
Or stay in our garden,
Laugh and make all sorts of plans.

When I saw you in passing,
Long ago now it seems,
I saw your lost little child
Deep inside your eyes.
I heard her say,
'Please be my friend.
I need your company
To share my days
And learn how beautiful
This life has always been meant to be.'

Join me in our journey.
I would love you here to hold my hand.
So could you join me in our life journey?
This one has no need for any plans.
It is the one we venture to any time we wish;
This one in our minds that reminds us how to live.
Come with me, my dearest friend,
So then we can always travel together
To those magical places that have no end.

Where we see all earth's beauty,
We now understand how blessed we are.
There is nothing that could compare.
Incredible times we will experience
Indescribable beings of nature
We are given to enrich this world.
Our gifts of creating from that which is,
Will be our solace for eternities.
Our gifts of creating from that which is,
Will be our salvation
Upon this road to sacredness.

I wait for your return.
Until then, my dearest friend,
These days shall shine a light
Within my heart
To feed my soul.
It will be that beacon throughout our nights.
Company of our minds
Shall grow as flowers in a quiet corner.
Until then, my dearest friend,
I wish.

Hemispheres of our universe,
I speak to you from my heart
To hear our humility.
It has seen what we have done,
And so too learnt to fear
Just what we have destroyed
With intent
Or with ignorance.
This earth has paid this price
While now we feel
The tide has turned
And we are lost.
So ask yourselves,
Will this lacking in your heart suffice?

Hemispheres of our universe,
I call to you from my heart
To feel our humility.

It has realised just what we have done,
So then looked upon that fear,
Painfully discovered just what we have destroyed
With intent
Or with ignorance.
Our earth has bled
From wounds of our selfishness.
She cries within the corridors of dreams.

Hemispheres of all that is sacred,
Universal intelligence omnipotence divine,
I beseech all that you are
With all that I am
In humility.
They that have understood;
They that wish to see;
They that have unmasked their egos;
They that have lost their ways
And wish to be home;
They that have given their wealth
To become rich from its sharing;
They that are creators,
Live to nurture and protect
Today and every day;
They that allow
All this world's magnificence
To grow and thrive.
They that give all of themselves
For our universe to survive.
In this surviving
We shall evolve into its light.
I wish this with all I am.

Universe of Colours

Flowers grow in my garden.
They look up at the trees,
Seemingly unaware of what they do.
But I have seen all the love they do bring
Without need for wealth.
They give without taking.

Colours so vibrant,
They can stop your heart from breaking.
And all the while
I smile while I sit in my garden.
We watch the world go by.

Flowers grow in my garden.
We look up at so many trees,
Aware of nature's sacredness.
I understand the love they do bring
Without need of wealth.
They forever give with no want to receive.

Colours that reflect our diversities;
They can rebuild your heart.
And all this while
I smile while I walk through my garden,
So we can watch the world go by.

Flowers abound in my garden.
We quietly look up at our forest of trees
In contentment in this knowing
Of their sacredness.
My heart is renewed,
For understanding this love for my soul.

I am a rainbow of love.
So all this while
I will smile
Whenever I think of my garden.
It is this place I forever can go to
When the world has forgotten to remember.
My space where I can cry;
My place where I can become.
Endless colours that make me smile.

Small Pieces of Sacredness

Pop the kettle on!
It's time for a moment to reflect.
If we don't stop now,
We have no chance to
Sit on our favourite couch.
Dip into the big tin that says
'Keep Out'.
It only really means
Until you are as full as a tin of beans.
With the chores and the boars,
Or another hectic day,
And you can see your will to live
Is slipping like a rug
On a highly polished floor.
Then the neighbour next door
decides to build an extension.
Oh yeah!
I almost forgot to mention!
The rain clouds have turned
Your patch of sky to grey,
And a familiar feeling in your head
Has begun screaming,
'What the Fred!'
So this impulse must be met,
Or you'll have to be seen by your vet
For howling
When the full moon is still a week away.
But that cavalry will arrive
Soon as I fill the kettle.

Breathe that sigh,
Scan the kitchen for that sacred sugar tin.
Mine is the size of a large shoe box
I used to use for my clean collections of socks,
Then questioned myself one day
As to the relevance of something so large
That would be an awesome receptacle
Just for cakes.
And you know
I never looked back
At that moment
When I cracked,
For it taught me
A lesson for life:
When you work and give so much of yourself,
You really need to stop,
Make a brew of your choice,
Then reach for your special tin.
Yes, that one with pieces of heaven within.
Put your hands together and look up to our sacred realms.

Awaken

In the soul of us you dwell.
Although I know you,
I can only but tell . . .
This sound of memories calling upon the sunset,
As all that is to be awaits.

A sacredness of light.
Here you have always known me.
Where time is but a lost voice,
There drifting upon an ancient breeze
Within all that is to be awaiting.

Still, where I am is now,
To see with strength of heart.
And all that was impossible to me
Has found me like a lost child,
So now this earth need wait no more.

For each day given without a recompense,
Is breath I dearly share.
Within our wealth of magic and misfortunes,
I shall always hold the light.

So that some may see.
So that some find freedom along their paths.
So that some will learn where life is love.
So that some have understanding that can surpass all
     wisdoms.

Inside this form,
This phantom of realities,
We have no more time
To shield our eyes from fears.

It is for us to walk among the fallen,
And there to find ourselves.
Despite our selfishness and greed,
We must hold the light.

For all who wish to grow this earth,
Wealth is giving.
So there upon such pain and poverties,
All shall learn upon this road
That there is no other way of living.

ORBS OF ILLUMINATIONS II

_____

This day was to be a most important day. Different from all the other different days that taught something about how to create lovely things within this world.

As sisters who were always loved and nurtured from before they were born, they learnt that whatever beautiful moments they gave to everything, every day, gave back beautiful moments that filled up their minds with happiness.

Today threw down soft, shiny sunshine. It poured through the towering, thick, emerald-green trees standing like sentinels around Ralphie's lush, multi-coloured garden. He barked with a cheekiness that made his whole face smile. There was no way of feeling sad or lonely once you entered Ralphie's back garden. He herded the sisters together with the gentleness and playfulness they knew so well as they laughed and skipped up the path trying to catch invisible fairy clocks.

Hours had melted into a day that these sisters would already have filed away into their special memories room. Then it was time for watering the vegetable plot set in the top corners of the long back garden, along with clusters of neon-coloured flowers that clung on to the lumpy, yellow stone boulders making up the garden walls. So many families of happy crawlies live there. When it rained, there was always a constant procession of beautiful and funny bugs that had somewhere to be, or just liked to stroll around in the raindrops. Some actually wore them to transport water to wherever stuff needed a helping hand. They used them as buckets! How cool is that!

Sisters of the most fantastical order, as these are, work together each and every day to make beautiful things happen. As you must have guessed, these sisters are the most beautiful sisters you could dream of meeting.

But, you know, what they had always known, through some magical something not known to humans who refused to give the best of themselves to everything they did, was that everything is here for a special reason. Just what this reason is did not need to explain itself to them. They knew.

From the days of their littleness, the sisters had an energy. Being awake was their reason to do lovely things in their little world. It was of no consequence if there was no reason. When a new day was peeping over the mysterious place where night met day, the sisters woke. They knew, with the millions of stars in their little beings, that whatever arrived upon their day doorstep, they could and would create wonderful things to make it shine. As babies they had a glow about them. Anything that came their way was of immense interest. While times were shrouded in grey gloominess, it took no time at all to change it to a brightest shade of happy you would choose in a candy shop. But yet, when others made no difference to their sadness of circumstances, the sisters had an ability to help them leave their sorrows and enter their incredible infantile innocence.

So the days only grew larger, sunnier, funnier. They had their own language, spoken without need of words. Words are beautiful things in the usual, unsuspecting, rough and tumbling day. Surprisingly though, words have been known to confuse many issues of confusing days. With an ability as theirs, working together as one entity was, and is, like a family of mice who have learnt to make their own cheese! Not only do they love their lives, they have learnt, as they have chosen to do so.

Growing into individuals, walking, talking, understanding their littleness in their big world that was everywhere, planting the seeds of who and what they wished to become, choice was always a friend that they knew, as if they had known it forever. Strange as you must think, choice is a force of nature given to everything, to a greater or lesser degree. Invisible, inexplicable, incapable of being anything but integrity of our sacred senses.

Along that fast and furious journey, from toddling to teens, these two incredible individuals were of strong character and so genteel, that others were of more importance than they allowed of themselves.

To see such determination, such selflessness, set in the biggest hearts of humilities was a unique journey in itself. Helping others whenever times came together in alignment would undoubtedly lead to miracles. Over many years of turmoil, loss of security and loneliness, the sisters chose to grow by planting beautiful seeds in their damaged garden, but they always chose to nurture each seed as best they could. However, to be lesser than they were was not an option they cared for. When moments unearthed the worst side of human nature, they always shone like the stars they are. Sometimes sadness of the cruel circumstances they had been trapped by had to be healed by just returning to this sanctuary of home. Home, where that one and only individual in this world lives, where that one and only being dwells that can rearrange your whole mind space. That one and only point of light, guiding you back to all that is sacredness. Silent, secure, your warrior of a thousand wars, where nothing fearful can draw breath and your universe is protected by the gates of this love that is eternity.

As you can imagine, as sisters they have different characters, but up to a point. There is an overlapping of each and every trait, where seeing one is knowing the other. I discovered this phenomenon, it seems, forever. It is something if asked they would deny. As someone close, I am constantly fascinated by it, by them.

Within their journeys from that place of dreams, along endless nightmares that I have torn apart to keep them safe and empowered with strengths I never realised I possessed, you see that the place I have journeyed from has empowered me with abilities only grown from a depth of understanding that is forged from lack of nurturement. Being loved, truly loved, is to be given all that you ever need to create beauty in this world. Being truly loved is when all that is sacred aligns in your being. To love with all you are is to create beauty that can only grow beauty.

Home time at the end of our day begins when the passage light bathes us three with its amber glow. Red rustic stone tiles in the porch lead us along the passageway, absorbing our tired toes. Hot, buttered toast wafting through our cold, damp noses explain that this is Friday. End of the hard-worked week is to celebrate without exception. Tonight we make a team-effort meal. When that feeling fills our eyes that shouts out 'I am just too exhausted!', we give each other a big hug and decide on what's waiting for us in our favourite takeaway. Soft light has snatched away all of the day's decisions, expectations and mental demands, as our table is laid with the rainbow-rimmed plates that we bought last Christmas at the local hospital's car boot sale. Tulip glasses snuggle in the centre, waiting to chime out thankfulness for everything. While the odds and ends are completed in the house, that fill the house with us and how fantastic we all are, foods are ready for us to come together in front of our magnificent flame-effect fire. Radio is playing lovely night music, just to let us know that thinking has finished for the day.

So much life to talk about since we left a few hours ago, that we are simply buzzing! We all agree wholeheartedly that it is nothing short of a miracle having our weekend ahead. As our laughter floats across the kitchen, we are all mesmerised by the little synchronised fairy lights that have appeared out of the dusk, like tiny tangerine stars. My girls had bought them from our local charity shop this afternoon, and while I was tidying up before our supper, they had set them up to create a beautiful moment for us all. We turned to each other with tears in our eyes and held hands so very tight.

***

Choice, you understand, is a unique but abstract concept for those who understand. So much can become so little in the blink of an eye. Life has no regard for your mindset or ego. Much can dismantle those paths that you choose to venture through. There is no certainty of circumstances, no stamp of authenticities, upon birth. It is all up to you when it comes down to it. The good times, the bad times, who and what you wish to be. But in the becoming, there is an unspoken story that only *we* have the power to speak.

Nurturing is reflected in all of nature. In the giving of ourselves to create and nurture, we are truly living within nature. Nature gives without taking. There is a synergy. We are here to complete that synergy that has always given everything we need to grow. Our world is given to us to create beautiful things every day. There is a way of being. We have the abilities to nurture within each moment. In uncertain times at best, frightening times at worst, we have a strength of character that has been forged by many sufferings. As nature does not waste, our experiences throughout life have no need to be lost without meaning.

Living life with that abundance of all that you have lived through evolves you into another realm of existence. It is not to be held in shame. It is our impossible legacy of wisdoms. We can choose to become alchemists of our own destinies, to turn all the sufferings into the most beautiful creations that will heal all that is. Oh yes! And the sisters? You guessed it! My daughters.

Barefoot Across the Moon

Mercurial seas
of silver,
Armoured waves
Glint beneath
Your gaze,
Silent amid
This hallowed sky.
Orb of sacredness,
Full with the dreams,
We brave.
We warriors
Of this Eden
Almost lost,
But where
This hope,
This heart,
Protects its beating.
All shall not be lost
In this place
That walks night
As a thousand shadows
Beyond depths of contemplation.
I see your light.
I hear your voice
Within the winds.
No time can tether heart nor soul.

I have become universe,
But it is where no mere mortals dream,
Where nothing can be
Destroyed,
Where nothing will be
Absorbed into the void.
For here is a place of sacredness,
With courage we step into the night
Beyond this realm of shadows
Into impossibilities.
For here we breathe
With love,
With impossibilities,
With belief
Of what we can achieve.
So now we need
Turn away from ignorance,
Abandon greed.
I look so far away to find you are there.
Hold out your hand,
Then I shall save your fall
And we can talk together,
Where dreams become reality.
And I am here whenever
You wish to find me,
Upon the shores of stars,
Awaiting wondrous things,
To nurture all that is.

Let our dreams allow us
To meet soon,
Walking upon
Our seas of dreams.
Walking barefoot
To feel our possibilities.
Walking barefoot
Across the moon.

For those who dream of possibilities
With all that they are.

Namaste.

Beyond Light

At some point in our life's,
We have a choice of direction.
Along those paths,
We can choose to see.
To see beyond darkest shadows,
We can create our terminator.
And in this choosing,
We alone have more than powers.
Our dreams are sacredness itself.
When we awake,
Our deeds will summon,
All the grains of our stars,
To nurture darkness into light.

Where life has broken us,
We must heal our wounds.
To understand these scars,
We need to light the way.
Stand strong amid illuminations,
Fear not our feeble limitations.
We are more than senses do allow,
It is for us to be as one sphere,
Become once more whole.
Where all has sheared into a million pieces,
We must find those which heal our world,
So there to heal our souls.
Magnificence has forged our universe.
Now our time has come,
'Let their be light'.

(Genesis. 1:3)

Lightning Source UK Ltd.
Milton Keynes UK
UKHW041337060622
403994UK00001BA/50

9 781789 632705